Artificial Intelligence Business

How you can profit from AI

by Przemek Chojecki, PhD

© Copyrights by Przemek Chojecki, 2020
1st edition

Edited by Katarzyna Mróz-Jaskuła, Studio Grafpa

Table of contents

Introduction 5
Why Artificial Intelligence 7
    Executive Summary. 7
    Artificial Intelligence Paradigm 10
    A short history of Artificial Intelligence 14
    Basic terminology of Artificial Intelligence 16
    Statistics related to AI 19
Practical AI and how it is done 26
    Research in Artificial Intelligence 28
    Open-source community. 31
    From research to applications 32
    Cons of using AI 34
Powering Enterprises with AI 37
    AI Maturity Levels 38
    Solving maturity issues 44
    Fostering a culture of innovation. 48
    How to shift an existing culture 49
    Hiring AI Talent 51
    Building an innovative culture in enterprises. 52
Boosting Startups with Artificial Intelligence. 53
    Make data-driven decisions fueled by AI 55
    Automate your marketing efforts with AI 57
    Improve your hiring process. 59
    Startups powered by AI 59

One person enhanced with AI 61
    One person startup 61
    Using AI as an individual 62
    Collect data 64

Trends in Artificial Intelligence 66
    AI in retail 69
    Manufacturing 73
    Logistics 77
    Robotics and Autonomous Vehicles 79
    Robotic Process Automation 85
    Image generation 89
    Text generation and Chatbots 92
    AI-powered education 95
    AI in Healthcare 98
    Cybersecurity powered by AI 106
    Climate Change 108
    Games and Reinforcement Learning 111
    Hardware and beyond 116

Machine Learning Trends 124
    Natural Language Processing 124
    AutoML or automatic AI 125
    One-shot learning and transfer learning 126
    Reinforcement Learning 128
    Computer Vision 129
    Fundamental concepts 130
    Pushing boundaries of machine learning 131

AI, Politics and Society 134
    AI for social good 136
    Public programs 138
    Ethics and Regulations 141
    Risks of using AI 144

Future of Artificial Intelligence 146
    We are all cyborgs 146
    Artificial General Intelligence 147

Introduction

We're living through a revolution. Artificial Intelligence is changing how we operate in the world and how smooth certain processes are. Just think about going on holidays. Multiple services allow you to find the most convenient flights and best hotels, you get personalized suggestions on what you might want to see, you go to the airport via one of the ride-sharing apps. At each of these steps, some AI algorithms are at work for your convenience.

I've started writing this book to fill in the gap. There are plenty of resources to learn machine learning and data science for technical people but no overviews, trends, discussion of applications, or anything at a more abstract level. On the other hand, those technical books are inaccessible to business people who don't want to go into coding themselves and want to stay at a more abstract idea level. The goal of this book is to address both issues and have a book that will be interesting both for data scientists and people with a business background.

That's why there's no code in this book, but I wasn't refraining from explaining certain more technical trends or discussing general toolset for artificial intelligence. The book is intended as a useful guide rather than a novel, that you have to read from the beginning until the end. Chapters are connected, but feel free to skip them whenever you want.

All in all, after reading this book, you'll know recent business applications of AI, understand how machine learning works and what to expect from it, what's trending, and how AI transforms every single business. Whether you're running a business, work at a large enterprise or in the public sector, this book will give you an overview of Artificial Intelligence as it is practiced today. I finish by discussing how we should integrate AI into our society, what are the risks of AI and how we can use AI to our benefit in the future.

Why Artificial Intelligence

Executive Summary

Artificial Intelligence is used in business through machine learning algorithms. Machine learning is a part of computer science focused on computer systems learning to perform a specific task without using explicit instructions, relying on patterns and inference instead.

Machine learning algorithms detect patterns and learn how to make predictions and recommendations by processing data, rather than by receiving explicit programming instructions ('if-then' loops). The algorithms improve over time with new data coming in, 'learning' through examples.

Machine learning is primarily used in:
– *predictions*: what will happen,
– *prescriptions*: what should be done to achieve goals,
– *descriptions*: what happened.

There are three main types of machine learning algorithms: supervised learning, unsupervised learning, and reinforcement learning.

Supervised learning uses training data and feedback from humans to learn the relationship of given inputs to a given output (for example, how the inputs "date" and "sales" predict customers' preferences). Use it if you already know how to classify the input data and the type of behavior you want to predict, but you want to do it on new data.

Unsupervised learning explores input data without being given an explicit output variable (for example, explores customer sales data to identify patterns and classify them). Use it when you want to classify the data, but you're unsure how to label the data yourself, or you want to discover hidden patterns.

Reinforcement learning learns to perform a task by trying to maximize rewards that you prescribe for its actions (for example, maximize returns of an investment portfolio). Use it when you have limited training data, and you cannot clearly define the end goal, or you want to explore possibilities without assuming what the solution might be.

The most common framework for doing machine learning is Python as a programming language. Experiments with machine learning models usually require access to powerful computers to 'train' algorithms. That's why the additional cost of doing AI is the cost of the cloud when data scientists train their models. Those can range from a couple of hundred dollars per month to millions of dollars, depending on how heavy is the data and machine learning architecture. For most businesses the cost won't exceed a couple of thousand dollars per month unless they want to invest heavily in AI capabilities and train their own models, rather than mostly use pre-trained, open-source solutions.

The most common architecture for machine learning algorithms is neural networks. You can think of them as Lego blocks of different sizes and colors that you can mix to build a specific construction. The basic parameter of a neural network is how many layers it has and how those layers interact with each other.

Deep learning is a subfield of machine learning which focuses on neural networks with at least 3 layers. Deep learning is the actual reason why AI is so popular today, as its applications in image or voice recognition are far better than classical methods. Neural networks combined with enough computing power give outstanding results on real-world data.

'Big data' is another buzzword used in the last decade often. Big data never had a proper definition, always meaning having more data than is possible to process using a single personal computer. That's why what we today understand as big data (petabytes of data) is far away from used to be big data just 10 years ago (terabytes) and how it will change in the next 10 years (exabytes).

As data is crucial for machine learning algorithms, 'big data' is coming back in organizations as a fundamental term to explore AI capabilities. Machine learning requires that the right set of data be applied to a learning process. You don't need big data to use machine learning algorithms, but big data can help you improve the accuracy of your algorithms.

That's why often it's not necessarily true that you need a lot of data to start experimenting with AI. Especially with the raise of reinforcement learning and techniques like 'one-shot learning,' AI is within reach for every single organization. The first step to benefit from AI is to prepare data by cleaning it and sorting it by human coworkers. Then machine learning engineers and data scientists will be able to take care of the rest.

INPUT	OUTPUT	APPLICATION
Voice Recording	Transcript	Speech Recognition
Image	Caption	Image Recognition
Recipe Ingredients	Customer Reviews	Food Recommendations
Historical Market Data	Future Market Data	Trading Bots
Drug chemical properties	Treatment efficacy	Pharma R&D
Transaction details	Is transaction fraudulent?	Fraud detection
Purchase history	Future purchase behavior	Customer retention
Faces	Names	Face Recognition
Car locations and speed	Traffic Flow	Traffic Lights

Artificial Intelligence Paradigm

Though it might seem like we've come a long way in the last ten years, which is true from a research perspective, the adoption of AI among corporations is still relatively low. According to some studies, only around 20% of companies are experimenting with AI. Most of the companies have only started to dabble with artificial intelligence.

This new era of information depends heavily on the knowledge, and we're currently missing a lot of experts.

There's a lot of fear and hype around AI, and it's crucial to have as many people as possible to know about AI in order to understand what's possible and what's not. Only an educated AI-wise society will be able to adopt the technology fully. The goal of this book is to make it happen sooner than later.

At business level decision-makers, project managers and executives need basic knowledge, understanding of the machine learning paradigm, which would allow them to apply practical algorithms to real use cases, driving business, and growing sales.

On the other hand, trust is a crucial ingredient in any system. Thus explainable AI, being able to explain why these automation systems, machine learning architecture, act in this way, will allow us to understand how it's going to affect all of us: co-workers, citizens, humans. For that purpose, we need to think about re-education when it comes to our organizations and implementing AI elements in schools from the very start of education.

AI will mostly enhance what we do on a daily basis. It's not going to be full automation most of the time, but an augmentation of how we do certain tasks and how we work. This way of collaboration will also require rewiring of how we think of machines.

That's why we also need to think about regulations. AI is the atomic energy of our times, and we can either use it to produce bombs or use it to produce energy. The standard paradigm of computing is based on 'if-then' loops. Coders give instructions to computers, supervising every single step of computing. Machine learning changed that completely. Coders don't have to code every single step to make the computer work. They can just build a general architecture, like a specific neural network, and supply data in order to 'train' this architecture - that is, let the computer system self-tune as it sees fit by analysing data. This approach is more similar to teaching a child a particular task or introducing a junior coworker to a particular business process for the first time. And as it is the case with children, it often takes time for them to grasp the concept fully. It's similar to machines. They need retraining and rebuilding parts of their architecture to excel at a given task.

Because of this shift of paradigm, it became possible to automate more tasks and business processes than ever before. You don't have to program every single step of the process, predicting at each step what might happen and how to react to that. You can leave many of those details to algorithms, letting them see data and decide for themselves in each case how it should be solved.

Of course, that's theory. In practice, things can get messy. AI is not a magic wand, and it doesn't solve any problem you throw at it. You need good preparation to really benefit from artificial intelligence. This includes:

1. Clearly describing what business process you want to automate or optimize.

2. Defining what the output of the process is and how to distinguish between good or bad results. If that's not possible, or if this is a continuous process without an end, then define mid-steps and mid-results that are anticipated.
3. Defining what the input of the process is, that is what kind of data you take into account when looking for the output.
4. Acquiring large datasets related to the business process. Cleaning it by removing unnecessary parts and organizing it in one place and in one format (e.g. .doc files stored on a cloud).

Having done this work, you're ready to start hiring data scientists to build machine learning algorithms for you. Often this preliminary work will be revised and enhanced with new data and new insights, but you don't have to worry about it at the start of the process. The crucial part for you, as an executive, is being clear about what business process exactly you want to tackle with AI.

Explanation of this new machine learning paradigm and how to apply it in business is the main reason for writing this book. I believe that understanding how data science teams work, how machine learning models are constructed, and what they need to perform well, is crucial to be competitive amid today's technological revolution.

It is also crucial for legislators, politicians, and philosophers to understand how the machine learning community operates and what is possible with AI, to make legislations and laws working for everyone involved. There's definitely too much hype regarding AI when it comes to how fast it will disrupt human jobs as we know them. And even though I believe that will eventually happen, what we should prepare for is the next 5-10-20 years of growing dependence on AI. Every job will be enhanced by artificial intelligence, rather than replaced by it, and we shouldn't be scared of it. Examples in art and video games show that perfectly. We can learn a lot from the way machine learning systems look at our world and how they transpose it.

The most important thing is to stay open, embrace new technologies, and learn constantly. After all, what humans do best is adapt,

A short history of Artificial Intelligence

The term artificial intelligence was used the first time in 1955 by John McCarthy, a math professor at Dartmouth who organized the seminal conference on the topic the following year. In 1957 the economist Herbert Simon predicted that computers would beat humans at chess within 10 years (he was slightly wrong, it took 40). In 1967 the cognitive scientist Marvin Minsky said, "Within a generation, the problem of creating 'artificial intelligence' will be substantially solved." Simon and Minsky were both intellectual giants, but they were wrong about AI badly. These dramatic but wrong claims caused various repercussions in how people in the second half of 20th century thought about AI: more as a subject of a science fiction novel than actual science.

The idea of an Artificial Intelligence, automation of certain repetitive processes, dates back to the Cold War when US intelligence was trying to translate Russian documents and reports automatically. The initial optimism of the '50s was then undermined by the underperformance of these early models and fundamental lack of progress past initial results. With a lack of optimism, funding was cut substantially, and the academic community turned away from AI, especially in the 1970s, when DARPA cut its funding. This period of lowered funding and loss of interest was later called the AI winter.

A renewal of AI came in the 1980s with LISP, a programming language, and LISP machines, computers optimized to run LISP code, which was the default language for doing AI research at that time. A couple of companies were producing those computers and selling them commercially with some initial successes, but eventually, they were overtaken by personal computers as we know them today. Again results were not good enough as to what was promised in research proposals. The second AI winter began.

The start of the new era of Artificial Intelligence is dated from 2009-2012. The community of AI researchers was steadily growing from the 1990s and the early 2000s, with larger grants and some interest from corporations, but the most significant catalyst for the current AI revolution came in 2009 with the creation of ImageNet, a large visual database designed to test image recognition algorithms on. Then on 30 September 2012, a convolutional neural network called AlexNet achieved a top-5 error of 15.3% in the ImageNet 2012 Challenge, more than 10.8 percentage points lower than that of the runner up, beating classical algorithms. This was made feasible due to the use of Graphics Processing Units (GPUs) during training, an essential ingredient of the deep learning revolution that was about to start. Suddenly people started to pay attention, not just within the AI community but across the technology industry as a whole and the current revolution began.

The ideas we use today in AI research like neural networks were to some extent known already 30 or 40 years ago. However, what was missing was enough data and enough computing power to process this data. Machine learning couldn't take off without access to large datasets, and thanks to the digital revolution we lived through in the early 2000s, suddenly many Internet companies emerged, older companies became digitized, and there was more data than any human could process. On the other hand, assuming Moore's law being true, the power of computers has been doubling every 18 months, reaching the necessary power to process big data as it was created, or at least enough of it to make neural networks work. And once that was established, everyone came to AI research again: governments, corporations, scientists.

Basic terminology of Artificial Intelligence

Let's now jump into basic terminology related to AI. When we say Artificial Intelligence we mostly mean machine learning - a domain of computer science that uses learning algorithms able to tune themselves on data provided by a user. The fundamental block of machine learning is neural networks. They are algorithmic systems based on simulating connected "neural units," loosely modeling the way that neurons interact in the brain.

As we have mentioned above, these computational models inspired by neural connections have been studied since the 1940s. They have returned to prominence with the rise of computer processing power able to cope with large training data sets and have been used to successfully analyze input data such as images, video, and speech. Deep learning is a subset of machine learning, where neural networks have many layers of neurons ("deep network"). The more layers you include in your machine learning model, the more computational power you need to train it. We talk about the architecture of a model, when we want to describe how many layers it has, how many neurons inside each layer, and how they are connected.

The most common neural networks appearing in applications are:

1. **Feedforward neural networks**: this is the simplest type of neural network. In this architecture, information moves in only one direction, forward, from the input layer, through the hidden layers (those between input and output), to the output layer. There are no loops in the network. The first single-neuron network was considered already in the 1950s. Advances in computing power and available data allowed this method to achieve great performance in the 21st century.
2. **Recurrent neural networks (RNNs)**: neural networks whose connections between neurons include loops. One of the most common examples of RNNs is LSTMs which are used in language processing tasks.
3. **Convolutional neural networks (CNNs)**: CNNs were originally invented as a superior neural network model

for handling cases in which the input data consisted of images. In 2012 CNNs were used for the winning entry in the ImageNet Large Scale Visual Recognition Competition, which sparked interest in machine learning again.

I also note generative adversarial networks (GANs) and reinforcement learning as two methods soon to be more common in commercial applications.

GANs use two neural networks competing against each other. They are often used for photo-realistic image generation: one network is trained to detect fakes, and the other is trying to fool the first one.

Reinforcement learning is an approach in machine learning based on giving rewards designed by developers to steer the machine into good behavior. Algorithms learn by trial and error. A notorious application of reinforcement learning is AlphaGo created by Google DeepMind, which was trained to play Go at a world-class level.

Any of these deep learning methods require thousands of data records for a model to train and achieve the desired accuracy. The authors of 'Deep Learning' book mention a general rule of thumb, that a supervised machine learning algorithm should achieve acceptable performance with around 5,000 labeled examples per category and match human-level performance when trained on at least 10 million labeled examples. Of course, it also depends on particular use cases and algorithms architecture. Sometimes more data isn't that helpful if you don't know how to feed it properly into machine learning models. On the other hand, sometimes machine learning techniques won't add more value than traditional statistical analytics. That's why it's essential to assess your level of technical development, look at your goals, and think about possible solutions without AI at first.

A lot of machine learning models used currently are trained through "supervised learning," which requires humans to label and categorize the underlying data. Nevertheless, the new methods like 'one-shot learning' show that in the future, we won't need that much data to train effective AI systems. One will need only a small set of labeled data and a good architecture in place. On top of that, autoML might improve AI even further without the need for human supervisors.

All that means that if an organisation wants to adopt AI successfully, it needs to start with assessing its technology stack and start by collecting data at scale. Linking data across various segments (customer, communication channel, platform) as well as controlling whether the right amount of data is given is crucial. A machine learning model can be 'overfitted' if it matches too well the test data but doesn't work in production, or 'underfitted' if it fails to capture essential features and thus fails to generalise.

Statistics related to AI

Following analysis done by AI State Index[1], let's review some statistics related to Artificial Intelligence, that will fully show

---

[1] Artificial Intelligence Index Report 2019, in this section we cite their numbers directly unless otherwise stated.

how important this market is becoming (or already is). It's crucial to understand that we are still early when it comes to applied AI, and most of those statistics will grow substantially in the upcoming years. The reason for that is most of the cutting-edge research is still far away from day-to-day business applications either because of the costs of the hardware or the required expertise to apply it. I expect the full AI boom to come within the next ten years when every company will need to implement AI elements to be competitive even at the local scale. This will come in pair with the democratisation of AI: the cost and difficulty of implementation of most algorithms will largely decrease. AI applications will be as available as general cloud storage is now.

Looking at Google Trends one can see that "cloud computing" appears in 2008 and then it is replaced by "big data" which starts taking off in 2011. "Machine learning" and "data science" begin to rise together in 2013, which matches the renewed interest in AI after the 2012 ImageNet competition.

Let's now look at different aspects of the Artificial Intelligence ecosystem.

Research

- Between 1998 and 2018, the share of AI papers among all papers published worldwide has grown three-fold, now accounting for 3% of peer-reviewed journal publications and 9% of published conference papers.
- The number of AI research papers surpassed 35,000 in 2019 worldwide as evaluated by looking at arXiv and AI

conferences. Most AI papers are published in North America and China.
- The number of patents related to AI is growing faster than the number of scientific papers. Most of the patents are within the computer vision subdomain and are registered in the US.
- Europe publishes the most AI papers. Papers published by American authors are cited 83% more than the global average.

Business and Funding

Global investments in AI and AI startups continue to rise. From a total of $1.3B raised in 2010 to over $40.4B in 2018 alone, funding has increased with an average annual growth rate of over 48% between 2010 and 2018.

'State of AI Report in 2019' claims that the number of AI companies that received funding is also increasing year by year, with over 3000 AI companies receiving funding in 2018. They calculated that between 2014 and 2019 (up to November 4th), a total of 15,798 investments of over $400K have been made in AI startups globally, with an average investment size of approximately $8.6M.

On the other hand, Crunchbase lists 13,650 AI companies as of May 2020, of which 97.8% are active. They have raised $19M on average, the median funding being $2.2M.

VC-driven private investments accounted for about half of total investments in AI in 2019, with M&A and Public Offerings taking the major share of the remaining half. However, private investment accounted for 92% of the number of deals, with M&A making up just over 4% of deals, and Minority stakes and Public offerings (IPOs) together accounting for 3%. These statistics show that most of the money goes to already successful startups.

"AI investment[2] is growing fast, dominated by digital giants such as Google and Baidu. Globally, we estimate tech giants spent $20 billion to $30 billion on AI in 2016, with 90 percent of this spent on R&D and deployment, and 10 percent on AI acquisitions. VC and PE financing, grants, and seed investments also grew rapidly, albeit from a small base, to a combined total of $6 billion to $9 billion. Machine learning, as an enabling technology, received the largest share of both internal and external investment." AI investments keep on growing in the last years.

Markets and Markets estimate that the AI market will be worth $190 billion by 2025.[3] We might hit this benchmark even sooner when you look at the above examples. To add even more examples:

- Open AI had a recent investment by Microsoft of $1 billion.
- SoftBank announces the second Vision Fund, which will be AI-focused and which will have $108 billion to invest.
- SAS is going to invest $1 billion in artificial intelligence over 3 years starting from 2019.

---

[2] McKinsey report on AI from June 2017
[3] https://www.marketsandmarkets.com/PressReleases/artificial-intelligence.asp%20.asp

The US federal government is projected to invest around $5 billion in AI R&D in fiscal 2020.

In the fiscal year 2018, the latest year in which complete contracting data is available, US federal agencies spent a combined $728 million on AI-related contracts, an almost 70% increase above the $429 million that agencies spent in fiscal 2017. Since the fiscal year 2000, the Pentagon has accounted for the largest share of AI spending of any federal agency ($1.85 billion), followed by NASA ($1.05 billion), and the departments of the Treasury ($267 million) and Health and Human Services ($245 million).

We can easily extrapolate that investments in AI and AI-related companies will only be growing in the next years as more research will be available for commercialisation. Also time of commercialisation might be shorter due to the growing talent pool and democratisation of AI.

Hiring

Hiring AI talent is hard, as the market is very competitive. Big tech companies have been actively buying AI startups, not just to acquire technology or clients but to secure qualified talent - this is usually called acquihire and is often practised in tech markets.

The pool of experts in machine learning is small, moreover, Microsoft, Amazon, Facebook, Google, and other tech giants have hired many of them. Companies have adopted M&A as a way to grab the top talent - typically those deals are valued at

$5 million to $10 million per person on an M&A deal (the lowest is usually $1 million per person). The shortage of talent and the cost of acquiring talent are underlined by a recent report that companies are seeking to fill 10,000 AI-related jobs and have budgeted more than $650 million for salaries. The US alone is opening over 7,000 AI-related jobs in 2019.[4] We can look at three aspects of the AI job market.

- **growth**: the rapid growth in AI hiring is also confirmed by job postings data from Burning Glass that shows the share of AI jobs (% of total jobs posted online) grew from 0.1% in 2012 to 1.7% in 2019 for Singapore. Similarly, in the US, the share of AI jobs increased from 0.3% in 2012 to 0.8% of total jobs posted in 2019.
- **demand**: machine learning jobs increased from 0.07% of total jobs posted in the US in 2010 to over 0.51% in October 2019.
- **salary**: compensation of senior engineers at large tech companies is approaching $1,000,000 of which about half is in company's stocks. At the other end of the spectrum, there's huge growth in $1.47/hour data labeling jobs.

All in all, hiring might be the biggest bottleneck for organisations to start deploying AI at scale. There are various ways to overcome this problem:

- outsource AI tasks to specialised software houses,
- use existing solutions and adapt them to your needs,

---

[4] https://enterprisersproject.com/article/2019/8/ai-artificial-intelligence-careers-salaries-7-statistics

- acquihire whole teams,
- offer a competitive environment for machine learning engineers.

We'll come back to these issues in the next chapters, while discussing how to use AI in organisations, be that large enterprises or startups.

Practical AI and how it is done

Artificial Intelligence in business is practical. When you think about neural networks, don't think about abstract mathematical structures, but rather computer systems that need data to learn business processes and how to operate within them.

Data Science is not a real science, it's an experimentation domain, where you need to constantly adjust, test, build prototypes from scratch, and rebuild what you have. It's a framework for approaching problems rather than a specific set of tools. This paradigm of using neural networks, statistics on steroids, is what makes AI both practically and theoretically complex, with such a broad range of applications, which we're going to cover in the next chapter.

So how Data Science or Artificial Intelligence is currently done? You could split the actual work into two parts, connected strongly with each other:

- implementation,
- research.

Implementation phase is focused on delivering practical solutions to a specific business problem. By using data from within your organisation, data scientists implement machine learning models to learn on this data. This phase is heavily focused on engineering aspects of data science:

– cleaning data
– feature extraction
– statistical analysis
– training neural networks
– setting up virtual machines and a general framework.

Research phase is about looking for possible tweaks, ameliorations, or totally new approaches to existing problems. It may consist of reading scientific papers, white papers from other organisations, browsing open-source code on Github, talking with fellow machine learning engineers, attending conferences. The goal is to broaden perspective and find new strategies to implement.

It's in general impossible to say what comes first, implementation or research, as the first steps of data scientists are often building the very first naive model, seeing how it works on given data, and then looking for other approaches and enhancements. For harder and more engaging projects, machine learning engineers might start with research, reading what's possible to find on a subject on the web, and only then choosing a couple of models to implement and try.

Nevertheless, data scientists spend most of the time in front of the computer, whether reading, writing code, or training machine learning models. What's often misunderstood in corporations is that usual sprints done in classical software development (lean startup method) are not always beneficial to finding solutions to more involved problems that require deep thinking. That's why the 20% rule of Google, allowing for 20% time off to work on software engineers' own projects, is so fruitful. Data scientists need to tinker and play around with ideas to boost their creativity.

Research in Artificial Intelligence

The research community in Artificial Intelligence can be split into three divisions:

- machine learning community
- ethics and social community
- business community

Machine Learning community is concerned primarily with research questions related to building machine learning models: from architecture through data to implementations. PhD in computer science or STEM field is necessary to participate actively in it.

Ethics and social community focuses on social ramifications of doing AI research and applying it in practice: from legislations to important questions or limits on what should be the goal of AI research. People in this community often work in social departments of universities, think tanks, or public institutions.

Business community focuses on applying cutting-edge research to business problems. Those may include manufacturing, drug design, cybersecurity, video games, and others. Researchers here work mostly at research labs of large organisations. PhD is not necessary, but often an additional advantage when it comes to looking for a job in those.

If one wants to become a researcher in AI, the standard road is via university, doing a PhD in computer science, and then becoming an assistant professor or a research fellow. Thanks to recent changes in how research works, for example how Amazon, Facebook, Google and similar large tech companies are participating in doing research, it often happens that freshly mint PhDs go directly to one of tech giants' research laboratories. It's also possible that they do simultaneously PhD and work at one of those companies which is beneficial to each party: a company sponsors a PhD, the university is relieved from costs, a PhD student has a job and does something relevant to the industry.

PhD thesis itself is a monograph discussing and solving an open problem or some case of it, using novel methods in an already established problem or inventing new problems related to existing knowledge. Some topics are more in fashion at a particular time than others and this relates to interests of particular professors or interest of the market (where the money is). Often during the time of doing a PhD a student publishes a couple of papers, which then consists of the main body of a PhD thesis.

For a PhD student, the most important is finding a good advisor with access to interesting problems, funds, and a research group. Interesting problems will allow him to do meaningful research, funds will allow him to travel to conferences and spend money on infrastructure, the research group will be invaluable for research discussions.

Going to conferences is a great way to connect with fellow scientists. The most popular and most prestigious machine learning conference is NIPS, Neural Information Processing Systems' annual meeting. The number of scientists applying with their papers to NIPS is growing by 30% each year, which also shows how lively is the machine learning community currently.

From the point of view of business that competes with academia for talent, the crucial aspect is creating a vibrant environment to do research in. Assigning free time to do any research is a good solution, but crucial is building a research group around a senior figure in the field. It was often the case that large organisations hired a professor from the machine learning department together with his PhD students as a way to start up a research community quickly. For example, this is what Uber did with poaching people from Carnegie Mellon's robotics department.[5]

A big problem for established institutions like banks or insurers is presenting themselves in an appealing way to potential

---

[5] https://www.theverge.com/transportation/2015/5/19/8622831/uber-self-driving-cars-carnegie-mellon-poached

machine learning employees. Crucial here is understanding that what's appealing to researches is being able to innovate, have freedom of thought, an atmosphere of openness, and hard problems at hand to solve. No one wants to be stuck with linear regressions all the time. It's often better to pose too hard problems than too easy problems to attract talent (think Tesla or SpaceX).

Excellent examples of good problems are on Kaggle (www.kaggle.com), where companies run data science challenges for their business problems setting a prize for top entries. Often these competitions are attended by thousands of teams. One of the most famous ones was a competition run by Netflix[6] to make better their recommendation algorithms. By putting the prize at $1M the competition attracted a lot of data scientists, put Netflix on a map of great tech companies to work at, and gave Netflix a lot of new research input relevant to their business operation.

Open-source community

Important from a business perspective and still largely underused by the business is the open-source community within machine learning. Much of research is available for free on GitHub, a repository of code, and can be picked up and used jointly with other pieces to build something unique you need. Never making a prototype was so fast and cheap as now. The open-source community is also an excellent source for potential hires as it accurately shows

---
[6] https://www.kaggle.com/netflix-inc/netflix-prize-data

what a given person is capable of by just looking at his or her code repository.

Business-wise supporting the open-source community has many advantages: access to the talent pool, staying informed about current research. Moreover, it can bring business leads. Recall the model of Red Hat which was responsible for maintaining Linux and then earning money via support and customisations. In the end, Red Hat was acquired by IBM in one of the largest tech acquisitions to date at massive $34 billion closed in 2019.

GitHub itself was acquired by Microsoft in 2018 for $7.5 billion,[7] and Kaggle was acquired by Google in 2017.[8] This not only shows how important open-source community is for business but actually that you can make a business out of open source efforts if you're able to deliver a great product and build a community of engaged users around it.

From research to applications

Having discussed how research is done in AI, it's now time to focus on applications. Assuming you already have a data science team in place and preliminary research on a problem you want to solve done, the next step is to gather and clean data. This process can be short if most of your business is digital with easy access to data, or long and painful if

---

[7] https://www.theverge.com/2018/10/26/17954714/microsoft-github-deal-acquisition-complete
[8] https://techcrunch.com/2017/03/08/google-confirms-its-acquisition-of-data-science-community-kaggle/

you have many sources to look at and data is far from clean (say, surveys of customers done in various formats). If that's the case, preprocessing is a task that would need a separate team to complete. It's especially essential for all the later work, so don't ignore cleaning data.

Applying research to business applications means using machine learning models on data coming from your business and measuring how well they behave compared to how you usually solve the problem at hand (e.g. time spent on a business process, marketing/sales, number of relevant leads). After receiving data, your team of machine learning engineers will put metrics in place to measure progress and start implementing (coding) machine learning algorithms, filling them with data you have provided. The end result will be either a metric of the accuracy of prediction, automated business process, or optimized computations.

What's crucial in the implementation stage is having good metrics to compare models (architecture), machines (infrastructure), and data used in training and evaluation. Understanding why the results are what they are is as important as arriving at the model yielding the best results.

Scaling the solution to more data and using models in production often requires more engineering than machine learning talent and thus requires hiring a different talent pool than in the research phase. However, as implementation and research are tightly knit, the best is having on board both researchers and engineers to work closely together.

ming up, practical AI in business is done through a cycle of:

1. researching possible machine learning models;
2. gathering data;
3. using models on collected data;
4. improving upon infrastructure, data, and scale.

After step 4, we come again to step 1, having feedback on how models work in practice and what can be improved, researchers can look for new algorithms and methods to tackle the problem at hand. The whole cycle is repeated until metrics defined at the start of the process are satisfied. That's why to finish the project successfully it's crucial to build a framework for machine learning experiments at the very beginning, even if it is to change later on with new experiments.

Cons of using AI

Using Artificial Intelligence solutions can create three risks.

Firstly, the machines may have hidden biases due to the data provided for training. For instance, if a system learns which job applicants to accept for an interview by using a data set of decisions made by human recruiters in the past, it may inadvertently learn to perpetuate their racial, gender, ethnic, or other biases. These biases are hard to detect as they won't appear explicitly, but rather be embedded in the solution where other factors are considered.

The second risk is that, unlike traditional software engineered systems built on explicit logic rules, neural network systems deal with statistical truths rather than literal truths. Thus it much harder or sometimes impossible to prove that the system will work in all cases — especially in situations that weren't represented in the training data. Lack of verifiability can be a concern in critical applications, such as controlling a nuclear power plant, or when life-death decisions are involved (healthcare, autonomous vehicles).

The third risk is explainability. When a machine learning system makes errors, as it almost inevitably will, diagnosing and correcting precisely what went wrong can be difficult. The underlying algorithmic structure is convoluted and depends on many factors, hard to unwind.

Having discussed risks, let us now discuss the limitations of AI. As every other technology AI has a couple of shortcomings, starting with data requirements and going beyond it, we can list four challenges:

The first challenge appears when we want to apply supervised learning and need labeled data for training. Labeling is now often done by hired annotators, and it can take time to prepare an adequate dataset. New algorithms emerge that require less data or use other tools to create labels by itself.

The second difficulty lies in obtaining data sets that are sufficiently large and comprehensive for training. This is relative to the algorithms we want to use, but for many business use cases, creating or obtaining such massive data sets can be difficult—for example, limited clinical-trial data to predict healthcare treatment outcomes more accurately.

The third challenge is explaining the results of complex machine learning models. Why is this decision suggested? Explainability is vital in certified systems like in healthcare or finances, where regulations play a significant role.

The fourth limitation is generalizability. Transferring knowledge from one set of circumstances to another is still one of the hardest machine learning tasks - and it is studied under the name of transfer learning. Lack of transferability means that companies need to retrain certain models and commit more resources to go outside of known cases.

Summing up, AI is a great tool for any organisation that can harness its power. However it's not a magical box that solves every type of problem, and often it requires rich resources to do properly, both in talent and in infrastructure.

Powering Enterprises with AI

In this chapter, we'll talk about practical steps to level up your organisation when it comes to AI applications. The strategy here is mostly adapted for large enterprises with enough capital and structure to carry out a plan. On the other hand, I also take into account that large enterprises are often slower to adapt, more decision-makers need to be convinced, and thus a plan to power your organisation with AI might be harder to implement. It's also definitely different than if you're running a smaller organisation or if you're a freelancer. I will treat these cases separately in the next chapter, Boosting Startups with Artificial Intelligence.

Let's now go back to enterprises. They are organized into departments by their core function, ranging from sales/marketing to customer service, product development, et cetera. Because each of those departments has a different goal and thus is optimized for a different function, it's worth first to analyze what level we want to re-organise with AI. Is it the whole organisation, a department, a single project? Depending on what you choose, there will be different obstacles, organisational change being the hardest due to inertia and lengthy processes involved unless you have already a great innovative culture at your workplace (I'll discuss that as well). Before applying AI, you need to gauge your organisation's AI maturity level.

AI Maturity Levels

Let's look at the potential steps you might take to apply Artificial Intelligence at your workplace and what challenges you might face along the way. Gartner, a research and advisory company, has defined maturity levels for AI adoption as follows:[9]

Level 1 - Awareness: Conversations about AI are happening, but not in a strategic way, and no pilot projects or experiments are taking place.

Level 2 - Active: AI is appearing in proofs of concept and possibly pilot projects. Meetings about AI focus on knowledge sharing and the beginnings of standardization.

Level 3 - Operational: At least one AI project has moved to production, and best practices, experts, and technology are accessible to the enterprise. AI has an executive sponsor and a dedicated budget.

Level 4 - Systemic: Every new digital project at least consider using AI, and new products and services have embedded AI. Employees in process and application design understand

---

[9] https://www.gartner.com/smarterwithgartner/the-cios-guide-to-artificial-intelligence/

the technology. AI-powered applications interact productively within the organization and across the business ecosystem.

Level 5 - Transformational: AI is a part of business DNA, it goes into every business process, and it is a natural framework to work with. Every worker knows the strengths and weaknesses of AI.

To that, I can add Level 0 - No Awareness, where there's simply no discussions of AI or AI-related solutions at work, and workers are not aware of what exactly AI means and how it works. Unfortunately, this is the most common stage right now, even among the largest organisations. Following a study by McKinsey[10] on Artificial Intelligence adoption, 53% of respondents are at Level 0, even though the studied companies were already more aware than most of what AI can do for them.

Fortunately, these statistics grow each year. Another study by McKinsey shows a 25% growth[11] in AI adoption across various industries. Some major criteria why this happens can be tracked to:

– the cost of implementing AI is falling with AutoML solutions (automatic machine learning) and easy to use platforms, which automatically analyse data without a need for a data science team.

---

[10] https://www.mckinsey.com/featured-insights/artificial-intelligence/ai-adoption-advances-but-foundational-barriers-remain
[11] https://www.mckinsey.com/featured-insights/artificial-intelligence/global-ai-survey-ai-proves-its-worth-but-few-scale-impact

- the general awareness of how AI can be used is growing with growing coverage in major magazines and newspapers.
- there are more and more data scientists and machine learning engineers available on the market, thus it is easier to find experts to work with on AI. Especially if a company is willing to hire an external team from a software house to jump into AI.
- the track record and business case studies are more widespread. It's easier for managers to see the real benefits of using AI in cases similar to theirs.

You can also apply the same levels of AI maturity to society as a whole. If you think about it this way, then we are currently entering Level 3 - Operational:

- There are numerous AI pilots going on around the world in each domain of our life. Most efforts here are made by private and public companies with substantial help from governments as well. Examples: traffic optimization, cashless shops, e-government, big data analytics.
- Many countries have already adopted AI strategies and approved a budget for AI solutions. Publicly administered funds are directed towards startups and R&D. Governments put money into universities creating AI faculties.

To achieve a higher level of maturity as a society, we need to:

- broaden the scope of AI education, starting with primary schools, introducing Python as the main tool for computer science classes.

- include AI and machine learning framework into education at business schools.
- popularise machine learning and data science knowledge among the general public, showing strengths and weaknesses of using AI, overcoming fear, and showing potential benefits.
- incentivise businesses to invest in AI solutions and use AI in their processes.

In general, I'm optimistic it's just a matter of time when we transition to the highest level of AI maturity as a society. Artificial Intelligence is such a transforming force, with a proven track record already that it's a question of when it will happen rather than whether.

Nevertheless, you can go into level 5 right now with your organisation by carefully planning and mapping your activities related to AI. There are two main tasks you have to do to start:

- assess the maturity level of your AI adoption,
- follow a list of recommendations to go to a higher level.

The first step is to assess the maturity level of the company by asking what the company is doing when it comes to:

1. team/people
2. data
3. tools for optimization and automation
4. vision and values

For example, let's say we are concerned with the Marketing Department responsible for Customer Analytics. Data-wise this means we will be working with the following data:

- customers' feedback
- effectiveness of in-store promotions
- planning and forecasting
- customer segmentation

The first step toward assessment of the AI maturity level of your company is to gather data from the department by asking your coworkers and looking through past projects. You should start by asking the following questions to assess properly how AI is used in your organisation.

Team

1. Is there a dedicated AI team working on machine learning and NLP algorithms: data scientists or machine learning engineers?
2. Is there a team of data analysts who analyses, cleans, and processes data?
3. Do some of the jobs/tasks at your department are tedious and repetitive? What's the biggest obstacle in automating them via AI?
4. Is there a person responsible for managing the AI team?

Data

1. How is data stored currently? Do you store it in-house or using external services/cloud?

2. What kind of data is currently stored?
3. Do you clean and process data in any way upon reception?

Tools

1. Do you use existing tools for data analysis? What kind of tools are you using? How much automation is in the solutions you're using?
2. Do you use any Machine Learning platforms to extract insights from your data? Which data do you submit to it?
3. Do you use algorithms built in-house by your data science team to analyse your data?

Vision and values

1. Do you think about applying AI to each new project?
2. Do you continuously try to improve existing processes by using machine learning algorithms and available AI systems?
3. Are there communication channels between the AI team and other teams so that AI can be easily implemented whenever needed?

Based on those questions, you will be able to assess the AI maturity level of the company by measuring it against Gartner's description. The answers to the above questions would certainly allow you to pinpoint the AI maturity level and moreover might indicate what you should do in order to level up.

We will now go through each level to discuss how you can level up, no matter what's your current stage. This applies to each department or an organisation as a whole.

Solving maturity issues

Let's now talk about how a company can transition to the next level, no matter where it starts. Building AI maturity is crucial in staying competitive in our digital world. Enterprises are challenged and beaten by technological startups because of a lack of innovation or a too-slow adaptation to changes. In this section, I discuss each level and potential challenges associated with it.

Awareness (1)

In order to ascend to the very first level, one should organize a workshop for the whole department about AI, machine learning, data science, and their potential use in real-world scenarios.

Potential challenges:

– educating staff of new ways of doing marketing,
– overcoming fear of AI and explaining it in simple terms to everyone.

From Awareness (1) to Active (2)

To progress past the first stage, one needs to connect the company's data to the system able to analyse data. This way, the first generic algorithms can be put into action, and the user will get first visualisations and preliminary cleaning of data. This can be an external ready-to-use system built by another company, more experienced with AI. Depending on the context, an enterprise can start with:

- social media monitoring,
- competition monitoring,
- documents analysis,
- invoice analysis.

Self-service analytics becomes a significant factor in making decisions based on data, as they allow us to observe threats and opportunities for growth.

Moreover, one needs to form a team of data scientists or programmers who would operate daily with external systems and machine learning models. At this stage, it can be done by hiring external teams to complete the first pilots and have a sense of AI capabilities.

The whole department needs a workshop to get accustomed to the machine learning framework and thinking about data and processes with an AI in view.

Potential challenges:

- finding talented people within the organisation or hiring a new team to use a machine learning system; can be solved using an AI consultant agency.

- learning to use external platforms; getting accustomed to new software is often hard; people need time and workshops to overcome fears.

From Active (2) to Operational (3)

Data Science Lead is hired to manage the data science team and introduce new AI experts, build a practice, and form a vision for future products.

The company starts using a machine learning/analytics system to experiment with machine learning models and extract data.

The company goes beyond analytics into more advanced methods like:

- NLP for analysis of customers' feedback,
- prediction of future customer behaviors,
- segmentation of customers into similarity groups using AI.

Potential challenges:

- attracting Data Science Lead is hard; one needs to spend usually a lot to attract top-notch talent and create an excellent environment for growth, which would be open and research-friendly.

From Operational (3) to Systemic (4)

At this stage, the AI team should work on their own algorithms, which then would be deployed within existing and new products.

Implementing a visual system for building models will allow for fast iteration, testing, and deployment.

There is an active communication channel between the AI team and the rest of the department.

Potential challenges:

- open communication channels between the AI team and the rest; the way to overcome it may be organizing regular 10 min stand-ups to ask questions
- expanding the AI team with machine learning engineers; hard to attract talent - if Data Science Lead is really good, he'll be able to do it though.

From Systemic (4) to Transformational (5)

The whole department is educated in machine learning frameworks and AI pipeline through a series of workshops, which are run on a continuous basis. This will provide broad AI training to the whole team.

To each project/team, there is assigned an AI supervisor responsible for thinking about how AI can transform a given project or change it substantially.

The company leverages the in-house AI team with its own solutions as well as available platforms/services and open-source code (GitHub).

Decision-making is based on data and is enhanced with AI.

Potential challenges:

- explaining how real AI works - without overhyping it and showing weaknesses as well as strengths; it often takes time to do that part (workshops, seminars, one on one meetings).
- building a framework for what is being done internally and what externally when it comes to data and algorithms; it takes an understanding of what the goal of the company is, where lies the competitive advantage, and what will be the most important in 5 years.

Fostering a culture of innovation

One of the key components of being successful in implementing AI at a transformational level is building your company's culture around innovation and AI in particular.

A culture of innovation means creating a culture where every employee feels he or she has some level of autonomy to think independently and find new ways to solve problems. If you're the one in charge, it means you should put forward your decisions, but leave an open window for new ideas coming from your team. Trust is important.

You should encourage taking a reasonable risk and allow the uncertainty of results if you want to foster innovation. Developing new ideas is an iterative discovery process and as such needs people and ideas to flow freely. Understanding that this does not always lead to a product is also a key. Failure is an important aspect of building an innovative culture. You can't hide failures. Instead, talk them over with your team. A truly innovative culture rewards people for their involvement in generating ideas and executing them, it doesn't just pay for ideas. You should think of innovation as a mindset and a framework for running a business process rather than an end goal.

Openness is another critical aspect of building an innovative culture. The innovative culture welcomes different points of view, different perspectives and seeks to associate disparate ideas and technologies into new products and services. You never should hear an argument "we've never done that before" as a way to shut down ideas – on the contrary, it should be considered a challenge worth pursuing in the innovative culture.

How to shift an existing culture

Changing a corporate culture is a difficult task, and it should be done slowly. Don't force it; adaptation to changes at a massive scale is always painful. It should be done in steps:

- create a vision for the future,
- describe your vision in a story and pass it to your closest employees,
- create a plan of actions you want to reward and how,
- prepare materials for your employees and the necessary retraining programs.

There's no change without tracking how employees answer to senior management strategy. You should hear feedback and act upon it to make this shift towards innovation as smooth as possible. In the end, there are three ingredients in shifting a corporate culture towards innovation:

- rewards,
- hiring,
- retraining.

By rewarding innovative behaviors, hiring new talented people, and expanding the skills of your employees, you'll be able to create an excellent environment for innovation.

We should remember that the emergence of AI in the workplace requires a massive re-skilling of employees at all levels, especially when it comes to:

- adaptability,
- social intelligence,
- communication,
- problem-solving.

Re-training of employees is crucial to implement hybrid solutions of people collaborating with machines on a daily basis. In some positions this is already common (think traders). Still, adoption of machine learning, especially the most cutting edge research, will nevertheless require new skills to use available tools in the best way.

That's why building a mindset of life-long learning (courses, seminars, books) plays a crucial role in creating an innovative culture. Moreover, it builds trust whenever an organisation invests in its employees and cares about their growth.

Hiring AI Talent

Often the most challenging part of executing an AI strategy is hiring talented people. There's a shortage of talent on the market, and the best are usually picked by Google, Facebook, Amazon and other big tech companies. Even large enterprises which are not strictly technological in nature lack talent. So in order to overcome this challenge, it's critical to understand how to attract talent to your organisation.

Computer scientists, in particular data scientists and machine learning engineers, are looking for an intellectually stimulating environment. More often than salary, what's important is the possibility to learn, solve creative problems and be challenged intellectually. On the other hand, the fewer meetings and administrative burden,s the better for them.

Those conditions often are hard to meet in organisations with a corporate, rigid structure. That's why changing your culture slowly to a culture of innovation is a necessary first step. And this has to be as practical as it gets. Focus on results.

With a culture of innovation installed, the next crucial thing is to have a clear cut strategy for what kind of problems you want to solve with AI. The more down to earth and practical it is, the better. You want to attract open-minded, hard-working, bright individuals, and for that, the best way is to present them with a meaningful challenge, something which is technically hard and something which solves a real problem at the same time.

Do research on various platforms about the potential payroll to see what you should offer. Then don't limit yourself to just posting job interviews, outreach to people you want to hire, especially to senior data scientists who always tend to have a job and are seldom looking for one (talent shortage again!).

Building an innovative culture in enterprises

Summing up this chapter, we have covered AI maturity levels and discussed how to progress to the next level, no matter where you start. It's crucial to become an AI-enabled company to stay competitive in the future.

A key component to progress in AI maturity is fostering an innovation culture. We've discussed how it's possible to change corporate culture. It's a slow and steady process, but it pays off in the end. An environment where innovative ideas are rewarded and not frowned upon is perfect for attracting top talent in machine learning and data science.

Boosting Startups with Artificial Intelligence

In the previous chapter, we have covered large enterprises venturing into AI, now it's time for startups and freelancers who want to use AI in their daily work. The main difference will be the flexibility and scale of operations. As a startup, you're able to operate much faster, making adjustments on the fly. Of course, the more people you have onboard and more decision-makers to agree with, the longer it will take, but generally, startups can deploy AI pretty fast (or any new solution). However, what they mostly lack is capital and data at scale, which more mature organisations have.

Use AI to improve customer experience

Customer service is one of the critical components of successful businesses. "More companies are realizing that delivering great care is not just the right thing to do; it also makes great business sense. Seven in 10 U.S. consumers say they've spent more money to do business with a company that delivers great service," said Raymond Joabar, Executive Vice President of American Express' servicing organization. "Service is an increasingly important competitive advantage for companies, both large and small, that make doing business easy and put their customers' needs first."[12]

AI-powered tools can help you boost your customer service in many ways. Chatbots handle more and more customer support communications. Chatbots are a versatile approach to customer queries, offering a quick response 24/7. Not only you can make your customer service way better and frictionless, but thanks to chatbots running 24/7 you'll be able to collect data about:

− customer preferences,
− customer demographics for further analysis,
− common customer issues.

Having a chatbot is often just a cost of a couple of days and a couple hundreds dollars to start with a pre-build solution by one of the chatbot providers. Chatfuel is a great example. They allow you to quickly connect a bot to Facebook Messenger and run the very first bot within minutes of using their service.

Chatbots can be used to help you sell more, for example, by offering discount codes and mentioning products interesting to your potential customer. There is great example of restaurant chains running chatbots which would take orders on Messenger. Fancy a pizza? Just type to get it.

---

[12] https://about.americanexpress.com/press-release/wellactually-americans-say-customer-service-better-ever

Make data-driven decisions fueled by AI

Analysing data is crucial for any business, and with AI you can do that much better and much faster. You can get insights into customer behavior and real-time information about market trends to make the proper decision.

Depending on your particular market, product, or service you provide, you might use data gathered via Crunchbase or BuzzSumo to track the flow of information, see how your competitors are doing, what is trending and adjust your decisions based on that.

If you're further along the way and have genuine, unique data about your customers, then it's time to start implementing off the shelf AI solutions for customer segmentation and prediction of growth/demand.

We're living in an unprecedented age of data when often it's just a matter of giving a process a proper framework in order to solve it by looking at the data. There are many data collecting solutions available on the market which you can use to enhance your own data. Data gathering and data cleaning is the most crucial task before approaching any machine learning solution, and it will allow you to use AI to your benefit.

You can enhance your data by:

- running a CRM powered by AI;
- have a unified framework for documents, customer data, sales, and any piece of information which your business is generating;

- running crawlers to scrape the web in search of data useful from your business perspective;
- buy data through commercial platforms;
- analyse social media data like Twitter;
- track applications and hiring process.

You shouldn't just rely on static reports and websites and be proactive when it comes to data. Current economy rewards knowledge and actionable insights from most recent data, especially when it comes to:

- how to approach your customers,
- what your customers like and dislike,
- what are general trends in your market.

Understanding trends will allow you to develop new products and services, as well as adjust existing ones. By understanding potential employees, you'll be better at scaling your organisation. We've never had such access to knowledge on the spot, live, 24/7.

For example, Coca-Cola has launched a new flavor, Cherry Sprite, based on the data they had collected and analysed using AI.[13]

You don't have to be a data scientist to understand data or use AI. There are many solutions for decision-makers, marketers, business officers, salespeople, and this list goes on. AI

---

[13] https://qz.com/1088885/coca-cola-uses-ai-robots-to-invent-new-sodas-like-cherry-sprite/

is penetrating every niche of every business, and it's worth searching on the web what's currently available. I won't list any solutions here as the chance is that by the moment this book is out, there will already be something new and better. That's how fast AI solutions are being built right now.

So have a look yourself, do a small search looking for AI-powered tools to boost your:

- effectiveness (CRMs, databases, calendars, AI assistants),
- sales and marketing (customer data analysis).

That's a start for looking further into AI, especially when it comes to forecasting. Forecasting means predicting the future through data analysis. Whether you want to project future sales or estimate market trends, AI can help you efficiently make the forecast, from supply chain optimization to marketing spend.

In order to truly use the power of forecasting, you need at least thousands of entry data points to be able to use regression and other algorithms for meaningful prediction. Machine learning solutions, deep learning especially, need even more data to take off the ground, and often those kinds of solutions are custom made to your specific needs. You can either hire data scientists or seek external help by hiring software houses specializing in machine learning.

Automate your marketing efforts with AI

Using AI tools to boost your marketing is another great idea for how you can grow your company. Currently, there are dozens of products on the market that will allow you to manage ad campaigns, automate email marketing (rasa.io, Mailchimp), or help you with content generation.

Tools like Curata use AI to help marketers find an interesting perspective on a piece of news and show its relevance to your company. The more content you can produce, the better outreach you will have, and that's vital for the growth of any startup.

Buying into AI tools and taking time to learn them is important if you want to be a cutting edge company. As a startup, you don't have to fight with legacy software. You can often start from scratch with a new idea, implement it, and see how it works. This is the most significant competitive advantage you have over larger organisations. Use it to your benefit by regularly learning about the new tools you can use in your business."[14]

You can use programmatic advertising to reach a broader audience base and improve overall marketing results. Then you can use AI tools, like Albert AI, to manage your digital ad campaigns:

— media buying,
— audience segment creation,
— cross-channel execution,
— testing, optimization, and analysis.

AI can also help you personalise your message. This is how rasa.io is working, trying to understand what your email newsletter subscribers click on, and what doesn't perform that well. It then gets better with time, proposing to users the content that is interesting to them from the sources of your choice. You end up with a more loyal user base.

Improve your hiring process

Building a strong team is crucial to the success of any business. AI can help with automating talent acquisition workflow, for example, by sifting through candidates and pre-choosing those best fit for a job. If well trained, AI can indicate which candidates have the highest chance of fitting into your culture and bringing necessary skills on board.

Tools like PredictiveHire can help you quickly evaluate a large number of applications and narrow down the list to those best suited for the job.

Another option is creating a survey for your candidates to measure their expectations against yours. AI can quickly categorize applicants and split them into groups based on their answers, thus saving you a lot of time.

Startups powered by AI

As a startup, you have a great opportunity to deploy cutting edge AI solutions and unlock the tremendous growth of your business. So make sure you:

- deploy a chatbot to boost your customer service,
- use business analytics tools to make data-driven decisions,
- optimize your marketing campaigns and ad spend using AI tools,

- write down your most repetitive and tedious processes and let AI do it.

All of these tools are easy to implement and start using. If you have ever used a Facebook Pixel for your website, then the idea here is similar - you want to gather as much information as possible about your daily business and analyse it. Facebook Pixel and Facebook tools allow you to optimize your ad spend on Facebook platform, but if you want to advertise on other platforms, you have to implement other tools. Especially if you're going to analyse data across multiple channels and verticals, just think about:

- ad spend vs sales,
- email newsletter subscribers vs sales,
- invoice analysis,
- customer segmentation based on messages, sales, and profiles,
- business processes divided into time/action framework and analysed.

Options here are endless and will depend on your particular business offer and modus operandi. It's important that you keep track of your data from the early days. As a startup, you need to act quickly to achieve top performance and be able to compete with established players in your field.

AI won't solve all your problems, but it will allow you to boost your business to new heights. Making data-driven decisions and automating certain processes will make you quick and efficient. Go for it!

One person enhanced with AI

If you're a freelancer, working solo, taking external projects, or if you're just an individual who is curious and wonders whether you can use AI in your life, this chapter is for you. The question is, how can you leverage AI as a single person in your life and your solo work, without engaging larger structures and organisations. Is that possible at all? The answer is yes.

One person startup

If you've read previous chapters, then you already know about maturity levels at organisations, startups powered by AI, and projects delivered faster. Now think about yourself as a startup. If you're yourself a freelance writer, content creator, or a solo data scientist, you have a product or a service you provide (content, code, support). So first of all, AI can help you boost your effectiveness with all the tools mentioned in the previous chapter about startups:

- AI assistant for meetings,
- CRM or a smart spreadsheet for keeping track of your projects,
- smart newsletter,
- audience analysis.

AI can even help you take your hobby to another level. Say you're into running or video games. You want to understand your best options when it comes to specific shoes or a particular genre of video games. Machine learning algorithms can personalize your recommendations. Algorithms that fuel Amazon or Netflix recommendations for you are available as a black box on commercial clouds of Google or Microsoft. All you have to do is choose a model you want to test and run it on your data. Initial setup might be a little complicated if you don't have a technical background, but after a while, you'll get used to it and will be able to use it by yourself. Hyperpersonalization is the way we will shop and make our choices.

A universal solution, which is less AI, more smart engineering, is offered by Zapier, which connects various services through their APIs. For example, Zapier allows you to connect your email with Google Spreadsheet to keep track of customer emails in one place and thus build for you a custom CRM in a couple of clicks. That kind of task can be engineered manually if you're a coder yourself, but you can save time by using Zapier.

Using AI as an individual

Let's get practical and zoom out for a moment. In general, Artificial Intelligence systems can help you:

– gather, organize and clean data;
– process data for useful insights;
– make predictions based on historical data;
– automate repetitive tasks;
– optimize computations and processes.

Think about yourself and your freelance work as a one-person organisation with a function to optimize (time, money, happiness). Then you can start dividing your job into smaller tasks like:

- outreach to customers through emails and social media;
- monitor social media, web services for particular information;
- extract information from news to attain your goal or know what's going on;
- meetings and calls;
- working on a project, researching new ideas;
- marketing.

If you split your activities into buckets, then you can think about how AI can help you with reducing the amount of work in a particular bucket. You can start by asking yourself these questions:

- can outreach be semi-automated? Can you automatically get a list of potential clients and message them through a bot, only later taking over a conversation?
- can you monitor social media and news through AI-powered tool which gather various sources in one place and allows you to go through all new data quickly?
- can you use a platform to keep track of news coming in, analysing live what's going on, what's there to observe?
- can you organise your meetings and calls in a more optimal way, by reducing the amount of time spent on travels and waiting? Can you analyse how much time you need exactly for a good meeting?

- what are the core components of a product or service you provide? Can you automate some parts of it?
- can you use a marketing platform to gather all your marketing efforts in one place and monitor them from a single platform? Can you use AI suggestions to optimize your ad spend, analyze your customers, and grow your sales?

I have formulated all the above questions in the form of 'can you' because the answer is 'yes, you can.' For each of those points on the list, there's a product or platform which can do it for you, automating and optimizing the process that you have to deal with daily.

Collect data

My final tip is similar to the one I gave for startups: collect as much data as possible and act upon it. Think about your freelance projects: who are your clients, where do they come from, what's the usual pre-sale interaction, and so on. Ask questions and collect data to see what's going on. Once you have enough of it and more than you can analyse yourself, start using tracking solutions: business analytics software, marketing tools, CRMs; they are all for you.

One person startup is still a startup.

It will be harder for you to deploy machine learning models at scale because you'll probably have less data than established companies, but any automation will significantly boost your performance. Just think about installing a simple chatbot on your website to collect data about your potential customers, or use automated tools to analyse your invoices. You'll be surprised by the results.

Starting early with AI is the best thing you can do. Implementing AI tools to your workflow is often more straightforward than you think, and it usually just takes courage to try something new. There are plenty of tools out there for your work because countless startups around the world try to innovate in every single business niche. So do your research, find relevant tools, and give them a try. Be open. If you have data to analyse and repetitive processes in your workflow, you can most likely use AI tools right now.

Trends in Artificial Intelligence

From a business perspective, what counts is how Artificial Intelligence can make you money. At this point in a book, I hope I've conveyed the general framework that AI is here to help you automate and optimize business processes with which you deal daily. It's supposed to make you faster, more creative, and more efficient in what you do, and by that, give you some time and money back.

In this chapter, I will look at various business domains and go through how AI is already used in practice. From the most striking applications in retail to healthcare and video games, we'll go over use cases that made headlines in recent years. Moreover, I'll speculate about the general directions of AI applications and how your organisation can benefit from them.

Regardless of your geographical location or your budget, you'll be able to use AI in your organisation thanks to democratisation trend within the community. Open-source code available on Github allows you to pick recent research, tune it quickly with your data, and start using it to solve your problems. The whole process is fast, especially if you know a bit of Python yourself.

Before diving in more specific domain-trends, I'd like to point you to general meta-trends that appear in applied AI. Those are:

1. Autonomous machines
2. Automated processes
3. Optimized processes with human supervision

Autonomous machines trend is about making real-world robots, vehicles, or otherwise constructed things into independent self-sufficient (to a large extent at least) beings that perform one particular task very well. The simplest example is iRobot Roomba, an autonomous vacuum cleaner, which is already widely used in American households. Or think about self-service checkout. In this category, we will have autonomous cars (e.g. Tesla) or autonomous sorting machines operating in Amazon warehouses.

Automated processes trend is to take repetitive processes and use algorithms to make them fully automatic. The oldest example of this is a calculator, which led to more advanced computing machines, and the automation of computations. More advanced uses are, for example, macros in spreadsheets or connecting various applications thanks to Zapier or similar solutions. The current work done in this space often goes under the name Robotic Process Automation, and some notable players are Automation Anywhere, UIPath, and Blue Prism. On the other hand, automated processes also encompass healthcare problems: from diagnostics to drug design.

Optimized processes is a category where machines are supervised by humans, and eventually, it is up to a supervisor to choose the optimal answer from insights provided. Great examples can be found in marketing when one wants to optimize ad spend and effectiveness, by automatic A/B testing, looking for patterns and insights in marketing data. Nevertheless, optimization occurs everywhere, from marketing to real estate, from retail to manufacturing, as we will see in this section. Optimization is the most common reason why AI is employed at all. Machine learning builds upon statistics using most cutting edge hardware to deliver outstanding optimization performance across a variety of fields.

All in all machine learning is driving changes at three levels:

– tasks and occupations, for example, using computer vision to free up radiologists' time in detecting potential cancer cells.
– business processes, for example, Amazon warehouses introducing robots and optimization algorithms to their workflow.
– business models, for instance, going from pricing for an individual product (song, movie) to a subscription model based on personalised recommendations a'la Netflix or Spotify.

We're still early in the process, and hence machine learning systems do not replace entire jobs or processes but rather boost and complement human workers. AI is applied whenever a task is tedious and repetitive and can be automated, hence freeing up human time. For example, chatbots used commercially in customer service are not meant to replace employees entirely but make them focus only on the most unusual cases where a personal touch is necessary.

This approach at the current stage of research is also the only one feasible in production, as building a technology that would commit no error is either too hard or too costly right now. Nevertheless, you should keep in mind that machine learning is an active research field, with thousands of researchers constantly trying to push the boundaries and breakthroughs are announced every month.

Thus building a hybrid workflow of human-machine interactions is the most effective way to progress and build a great company in the age of AI.

Let's now focus on particular use cases of AI in various business domains. This list is far from comprehensive, but I just wanted to show what's possible. The chances are that some applications are already outdated. Our level of progress is so fast that by the moment you read these words, many more applications will emerge, which are even more amazing.

AI in retail

The sale of goods is a prototype of all human economic endeavors. AI plays already a prominent role in boosting sales of virtually any item, be it online or offline. Just think about the following use cases:

- classifying customers based on their purchase history;
- personalization of offer for each potential customer;
- analysing demographics and proposing an individual message for each customer;
- automation of sales via in-store technology;

- customer service done by chatbots;
- analysing competitors live 24/7 and reacting to changes fast;
- optimising ad spend and marketing campaigns;

to name just a few more basic ones. They are all related to smart analytics, and while they existed before the technological revolution, AI allowed retailers to boost analytics in a tremendous way. It gave companies tools to analyse and act upon insights 24/7, perform hyper-personalization, and considerably lower the cost of operating a retail business.

In January of 2018, Amazon opened its first high-tech grocery store[14] that does not require a traditional checkout. Amazon Go is an experimental grocery in Seattle, which allows shoppers to take goods off shelves and just leave without checkout. Computer vision identifies them as they enter the store, then links them with products taken from shelves. When shoppers leave, the system deducts the cost of the items in their bag from their Amazon accounts and sends an email receipt.

Enhanced user experience is the area that offers probably the most futuristic perspectives for AI in retail. Deep learning and computer vision technologies also will help store owners compete with the one-click convenience of online retailers by eliminating checkout altogether. Cashless shops around the world, especially in China are becoming more popular.

---

[14] https://www.cbc.ca/news/technology/amazon-go-grocery-store-1.4497862

Navigating a hardware store can be difficult, and that's why in 2016, Lowe's introduced LoweBot,[15] an autonomous retail service robot, in Lowe's Stores in the San Francisco Bay area. LoweBot was able to find products in multiple languages and help customers effectively navigate the store.

As LoweBot helps customers with simple questions, it enables employees to spend more time offering their expertise and specialty knowledge to customers. LoweBot also assisted with inventory monitoring in real-time, which helped detect patterns that might guide future business decisions

Sephora[16] has installed an AI-powered mirror in its store in Madrid to come up with recommendations for customers. The mirror detects data about the shopper looking into it, including gender, age, look, and clothing, and uses those points to recommend makeup, skincare, and fragrance offerings that best match the shopper's needs.

Airlines like KLM started introducing chatbots to help with orders. You can meet KLM's BB[17] on Messenger or through the Google Assistant to find a destination and book a flight.

Similarly, companies in other niches experiment with ordering through a chatbot for a couple of years already. Pizza Hut

---

[15] http://www.lowesinnovationlabs.com/lowebot
[16] https://retailtouchpoints.com/topics/customer-experience/ai-powered-digital-mirror-reads-sephora-shoppers-look
[17] https://bb.klm.com/en

was one of the first companies to introduce online ordering through Facebook.[18]

The Olay Skin Advisor[19] offers a web-based skin analyst application and advisor tool that uses artificial intelligence to create a personalized beauty experience once a user uploads a picture of their face (a selfie). The app evaluates skin health and makes recommendations for problem areas with personalised skincare regimen recommendations.

A great example of how AI is applied in business is done by Starbucks. Starbucks' CEO Kevin Johnson talked about Deep Brew, an in-house AI solution[20]:

"Deep Brew will increasingly power our personalisation engine, optimise store labor allocations, and drive inventory management in our stores. We plan to leverage Deep Brew in ways that free up our partners so that they can spend more time connecting with customers. Deep Brew is a key differentiator for the future, as we continue our quest to build world-class AI capabilities, to better support partners."

This Deep Brew technology is used in automatic espresso machines, to make the best coffee possible. Starbucks has also implemented chatbots in their My Barista App.

---

[18] https://venturebeat.com/2016/07/12/pizza-hut-launches-chatbot-for-ordering-pizzas-asking-about-anchovies/
[19] https://www.vision-systems.com/boards-software/article/14039551/olay-skin-advisor-smartphone-app-uses-computer-vision-and-deep-learning
[20] https://marketingtechnews.net/news/2019/nov/04/deep-brew-starbucks-aims-use-ai-more-humanised-customer-experience/

Another example of an enterprise applying AI comes from H&M,[21] which created its AI department in 2018 and has been since working on using AI in different segments. Most profoundly, it changed supply-chain. Forecasting demand is crucial for H&M to lower costs of operations.

Summing up, AI can be used in retail to evaluate demand at restaurants or other shops based on time or weather. Smart analytics can improve customer experience and suggest changes, increasing profitability. In-store virtual assistants can identify returning customers using facial recognition, analyze their shopping history, and make suggestions via a chat.

Online retailers are going for personal recommendations to customers, the more, the better. They are ahead in targeted marketing thanks to data gathered online. However, also traditional retailers have started to collect data from physical stores and then analyse it using data science solutions.

The future of retail is in hyperpersonalisation and data-driven decision making.

Manufacturing

Manufacturing produces 16% of global GDP, and for that reason, AI can hugely benefit the whole economy if it can boost manufacturing. And it seems like this is the case. I will divide manufacturing into:

---

[21] https://www.supplychaindive.com/news/HM-AI-supply-chain-sustainable/570400/,

- predictive maintenance,
- forecasting demand,
- factories (also partially covered in chapter about robots),

and discuss each use case below. The term Industry 4.0 emerged in 2011 to address the trend of total automatization of manufacturing. As a business vertical manufacturing is very susceptible to automation - many factories have already implemented automation to a large degree. Due to the digitization of manufacturing, it's easy to enter with AI tools and try to optimize processes. However, the most difficult challenge lies in using AI in the way which won't make errors in scenarios where errors would cost too much (human lives).

Predictive maintenance

Maintenance is a critical area that can drive significant cost savings and production value around the world. The cost of machine downtime is high: according to the International Society of Automation, $647 billion is lost each year globally.

Predictive maintenance is about detecting anomalies. Deep learning, thanks to its capabilities to analyse vast volumes of data, can take existing preventive maintenance systems to a new level. AI's ability to predict failures and allow planned interventions can be used to reduce downtime and operating costs while improving production yield.

This kind of solution is, for example, offered by Uptake or Dataiku. Both companies specialise in industrial applications of AI.

Forecasting demand

Hedge funds have been using machine learning to forecast demand for quite some time in order to predict demand for a given commodity. With more information available digitally, it becomes possible to use machine learning to forecast demand beyond finance and hence enhance any business by reducing waste and increasing profitability. For example, grid scale electricity is currently hard to store. This creates a substantial economic and environmental cost for both underestimating demand (blackouts) and overestimating demand (wasted energy).

DeepMind, a subsidiary of Google, managed to reduce wasted energy in Google's data centers by 40% by using machine learning algorithms.[22] Smart grids, combining AI with expert knowledge, are still in development, with many challenges ahead[23].

On the other hand predicting demand for retail purposes, like, for example, H&M we mentioned, is much easier to implement. In general, the more digital the process, the easier it is to optimise it using AI.

You can find many tools powered by AI, which are suitable for forecasting demand like FuturePlanning or Pipedrive. Often a

---
[22] https://deepmind.com/blog/article/deepmind-ai-reduces-google-data-centre-cooling-bill-40
[23] https://www.utilitydive.com/news/how-does-ai-improve-grid-performance-no-one-fully-understands-and-thats-l/566997/

good CRM with AI capabilities can significantly increase your productivity.

Factories

Factories are at the core of the industrial revolution, and it's the same for Industry 4.0 movement. The future of intelligent manufacturing lies in using machine learning together with experts' knowledge.

At Siemens' Electronic Works Amberg,[24] about 50 million items of processes and product data need to be evaluated and used for optimization for production to run smoothly. With Edge Computing, data can be immediately processed where it's generated, right at the plant or machine. People manage and control the production of programmable logic circuits through a virtual factory that replicates the factory floor.

The Nanjing[25] factory is part of Ericsson's global supply chain set up. State-of-the-art cellular IoT technologies in the Nanjing factory enable an automated alert system for the immediate attention of critical issues and faults. Implemented at 45 work stations, it allows increased efficiency and speed of the production system.

---

[24] https://new.siemens.com/global/en/company/stories/industry/electronics-digitalenterprise-futuretechnologies.html
[25] https://www.ericsson.com/en/press-releases/2019/9/ericsson-automated-smart-factory-operational-in-china

China is also investing massively in AI factories. MEGVII[26] is one of the very few companies in the world that have developed proprietary deep learning frameworks in this space. Their solution Brain++ functions as a unified underlying architecture and provides critical support for algorithm training and model improvement processes. Brain++ enables a customer to build a semi-automatic algorithm production line that is continuously self-improving and becoming more automatic over time.

This is just the tip of an iceberg as factories throughout the world are massively experimenting with AI-powered production lines, achieving significant increases in productivity.

Logistics

Machine learning algorithms can learn how to optimally allocate resources, like fleets of vehicles, to address dynamically changing demand (e.g. passenger requests) while maximising resource utilisation. Thus it's no surprise that logistics is another domain with AI adoption in progress.

In general, AI can help logistics in:

- demand forecasting,
- assisting last-mile delivery (from chatbots to autonomous drones),
- real-time decision making,
- creating contingency plans,
- tracking movement.

---

[26] https://megvii.com/en/about_megvii

Rolls-Royce[27] is working with Intel to develop self-driving ships. Rolls-Royce released the Intelligence Awareness system in 2018, a system that can classify all the nearby objects under the water. It can also monitor the engine condition and recommend the best routes.

DHL[28] has developed a machine learning-based tool to predict transit time delays of air freight to enable proactive mitigation. By analyzing 58 different parameters of internal data, the machine learning model can predict if the average daily transit time for a given lane is expected to rise or fall up to a week in advance. Furthermore, this solution can identify the top factors influencing shipment delays, including temporal factors like departure day or operational factors such as airline on-time performance. This can help air freight forwarders plan ahead by removing subjective guesswork around when or with which airline their shipments should fly.

UPS saves 10 million gallons of fuel per year by optimizing routes with surprising 'don't turn left' strategy.[29]

Satellite imagery company DigitalGlobe delivers high-resolution pictures of the planet's surface to Uber. These images provide rich input sources for the development of advanced mapping tools to increase the precision of pick up, navigation, and drop off between its drivers and riders. DigitalGlobe's

---

[27] https://supplychainbeyond.com/artificial-intelligence-in-the-logistics-industry/
[28] DHL, Artificial Intelligence Trends in Logistics, 2018
[29] https://theconversation.com/why-ups-drivers-dont-turn-left-and-you-probably-shouldnt-either-71432

satellites can decipher new road-surface markings, lane information, and street-scale changes to traffic patterns before a city adds them to its official vector map. This level of detail from satellite imagery can provide valuable new insights to planning and navigating routes not only for the transport of people but for shipments as well.

Startups like Transmetrics and ClearMetal are offering their AI tools for logistics to Fortune 500 companies and beyond, enabling supply chain organizations to optimize logistics and provide their customers with easy access to trusted, live information about their shipments.

Robotics and Autonomous Vehicles

Media and science fiction movies love stories about autonomous conscious robots taking control of the world. This vision is far from reality, and in this chapter, I will cover commercial use cases of robotics.

The most vivid imagery for robots is created by Boston Dynamics. Boston Dynamics has made tremendous progress in the last ten years, from barely walking robots to parkour performing athletic robots able to walk and run on any terrain. Each year they present innovation, and then there's a bit of public concern about the potential use of those in military missions.

However, the reality for robots is usually more boring as they are widely used for warehousing and logistics tasks.

Warehouse robots

Tractica Research[30] estimates that the worldwide sales of warehousing and logistics robots will reach $22.4 billion by the end of 2021. Robots are locating, tracking, and moving inventory inside warehouses; they are conveying and sorting oversized packages at ground distribution hubs.

Autonomous workers in Amazon Warehouses is one example. Amazon employs over 200,000 robots in its warehouses today, which is doubling from year to year. These robots service fulfillment and sorting, completing these jobs faster and better than human workers would. Amazon builds whole technology around helping robots navigate simultaneously in a cramped warehouse environment with QR codes and blocking sunlight.

Moreover, Amazon works on autonomous drones that would deliver parcels to secluded locations. In 2016 Amazon announced a partnership with the UK government, and it also works with the US government.[31] Amazon Prime Air plans to use the aircraft to establish a package delivery operation in the United States.

Ocado, a UK online supermarket, often grabs media attention with new implementations of AI and robotics at its core operations. Machine learning algorithms steer thousands of products over a maze of conveyor belts and deliver them to humans just in time to fill shopping bags. When fully operational, Ocado's

---

[30] https://tractica.omdia.com/research/warehousing-and-logistics-robots/
[31] https://www.bbc.co.uk/news/technology-48536319

hive of robots will be processing 3.5 million items or around 65,000 orders every week. The tasks being undertaken by Ocado's robots are very basic, and they can be expressed in one word — "lifting," "moving," "sorting." Thus we can expect to see the application of these sorts of robots also in other industries.[32]

Autonomous robots also work alongside people to increase productivity and reduce injuries. Swisslog's robot-based solutions combine KUKA robots and Swisslog's intralogistics know-how. They are designed to reduce operational costs and improve warehouse efficiency.[33]

DHL constantly tries to collaborate with various companies and push the research boundaries themselves.[34] In 2016 they unleashed a pair of fully automated trolleys that follow pickers through the warehouse and relieve them of physical work. Similarly, LocusBots from U.S.-based Locus Robotics are self-guiding vehicles that navigate autonomously around a warehouse carrying standard plastic tote bins. A display on the bot tells nearby warehouse associates what to pick for each bin, and a scanner confirms each item as it is loaded. By allowing workers to spend more time picking and less walking the aisles, Locus says that its system can double worker productivity.

---

[32] https://www.theverge.com/2018/5/8/17331250/automated-warehouses-jobs-ocado-andover-amazon
[33] https://www.swisslog.com/en-us/products-systems-solutions/picking-palletizing-order-fulfillment/robot-based-robotics-fully-automated
[34] https://www.dhl.com/global-en/home/about-us/delivered-magazine/articles/2019/issue-2-2019/robotics-changing-world-warehouses.html

Chuck[35], created by 6 River Systems, uses machine learning to help associates work faster. Chuck leads warehouse associates through their work zones to help them minimize walking, stay on task, and work more efficiently. It can be used in all put-away, picking, counting, replenishment, and sorting tasks.

Brain Corp. signed a deal with Walmart to scale up from an initial 360 robotic floor cleaner trial and add 1,500 more robots.[36] BrainOS, built by Brain Corp., is a cloud-connected operating system for commercial autonomous robots. Robots powered by BrainOS navigate autonomously, avoid obstacles, adapt to changing environments, manage data, generate reports, and seamlessly interact with end-users and other robots.

Berkshire Grey combines AI and robotics to automate omni-channel fulfillment for retailers, e-commerce, and logistics enterprises. In 2020 they announced securing a $263 million funding in series B led by SoftBank.[37]

China is heavily investing in AI, especially when it comes to manufacturing, logistics, and robotics. JD.com, the logistics giant from China, unveiled in 2018 a warehouse that can handle 200,000 orders a day but employs just four people – with their jobs centered around servicing the robots that run the place.

---

[35] https://6river.com/meet-chuck/
[36] https://www.braincorp.com/newsroom/brain-corp-to-expand-ai-services-in-retail-industry
[37] https://venturebeat.com/2020/01/21/berkshire-grey-raises-263-million-for-industrial-robots/

This all shows that the robotization trend is growing: 35,880 robots were added to U.S. factories in 2018, 7% more than in 2017.[38] And as we can see, not only warehouses employ robots. Logistic companies are also investing in implementing robots in their tasks.

We can expect an even larger increase of automated factories and warehouses as technology progresses and cuts down some of the costs. Within 10 years 90% of warehouses and factories may be entirely automated with a couple of human staff per building to oversee robots.

Autonomous cars

Autonomous cars are another hot topic when it comes to automation and autonomy. Many companies are receiving permits to ride their passengers in autonomous vehicles.[39] Tesla, Uber, and Lyft are already making tests on autonomous cars driving around California in 2019 and 2020.

California was the first state in the US with autonomous vehicle testing regulations. Ten states have authorized the full deployment of autonomous vehicles without a human operator, including Nevada, Arizona, or Texas. Some states like South Carolina, Kentucky, and Mississippi, already regulate truck platooning.

---

[38] State of AI report, 2019.
[39] https://techcrunch.com/2020/02/24/cruise-can-now-transport-passengers-in-self-driving-cars-in-ca/

In 2018 California licensed testing autonomous vehicles for over 50 companies and more than 500 autonomous vehicles (AV) - which summarily drove over 2 million miles. In 2018 AVs in California had 46 crashes noted as being in the autonomous mode when the collision occurred.

In general, the California Public Utilities Commission gives permits as a part of the state's Autonomous Vehicle Passenger Service pilot. As part of the program, companies must provide data and reports to the CPUC regarding any incidents, the number of passenger miles traveled, and passenger safety protocols. Companies must also have a safety driver behind the wheel and not charge passengers for rides.

The number of companies that were accepted into a program is growing.

Similar tests are performed around the world. The first driverless bus is already cruising in Singapore.[40] China, Japan, and Singapore are especially keen on pushing autonomous vehicles. Europe is catching up with Scania and Volvo, each producing their own autonomous buses and deploying them in their respective countries.

Moreover, there are more tests of autonomous trucks. The headlines were made by Otto, which were later bought by Uber. However, it still seems early for commercial use at scale.

---

[40] https://www.sustainable-bus.com/smart-mobility/autonomous-bus-public-transport-a-driverless-future-ahead-pilots-are-multiplying/

The crucial thing when it comes to training autonomous vehicles is mileage. After "State of AI report 2019" we can cite that: Waymo drove more than 1 million miles in 2018, 2.8 times next best (GM Cruise), and 16 times third best (Apple). The average Californian drives 14,435 miles per year. Only 11 out of 63 companies with DMV approval drove more than this in 2018. Self-driving mileage accrual in California is still microscopic when compared to all drivers. In total self-driving car companies racked up 0.00066% of the miles driven by humans in California in 2018.

This all means there's still a way to go for autonomous vehicles, and we shall see it unfold in this decade. When it comes to AVs and their use in commerce - be it passenger rides or transportation - the largest obstacles lie in creating suitable legislation and a proper environment for deploying autonomous cars on our streets.

Robotic Process Automation

A report by McKinsey Global Institute called "A Future That Works: Automation, Employment, and Productivity"[41] predicts that nearly half of work tasks will be performed by some form of a robot by the year 2055. AI agents will automate any kind of job that is repetitive on various levels.

---

[41] https://www.mckinsey.com/~/media/mckinsey/featured%20insights/Digital%20Disruption/Harnessing%20automation%20for%20a%20future%20that%20works/MGI-A-future-that-works-Executive-summary.ashx

I genuinely believe that. Not only repetitive tasks will be automated but also creative ones, as we can judge by recent breakthroughs in text understanding.

Robotic Process Automation (RPA) software is a fundamental piece of automation. RPA, at its core, is just an approach to automating business processes through the deployment of bots or AI. It dates back to the 90s, and back then, it was a purely software engineering task of breaking down a process into smaller pieces and connecting various APIs to replace humans. For example, having to copy a particular text from one document to another and then sending it through email. Though useful, it was primarily concerned with boring, repetitive tasks that could be automated by writing 'if-then' instructions.

Everything changed with the advent of AI. Now software is able to deal with anomalies, previously unseen cases, and make a decision for itself on the spot. Enhanced with text understanding algorithms RPA software is capable of taking upon more complex business process and don't need to be always guided by human labeling of every possible scenario. We're entering a new age of automation. We should expect even more disruption once reinforcement learning methods will be implemented within RPA software, which would allow for automating entire office jobs.

Let's review the most popular RPA solutions on the market right now.[42] Most of the companies have been around for over 10 years and became quite mature organisations.

---

[42] https://www.gigabitmagazine.com/top10/top-10-rpa-companies,

Automation Anywhere empowers people to focus on the work that makes their companies great with robotic process automation that automates virtually anything. Automation Anywhere operates a Bot Store – a marketplace for pre-existent bots suited for different roles. These "Digital Workers" are given job titles by the company, for example, "Digital Employee Onboarding Specialist" with tasks such as identify, shortlist, and onboard candidates. Originally founded in 2003 as Tethys Solutions, the company acquired its current name in 2010, emphasising its focus on robotic process automation.

Blue Prism is a UK RPA platform with customers like eBay, the NHS, and Walgreens. Its intelligent RPA platform comes in both on-premise and SaaS varieties (as most mature RPA solutions), working with the public sector, manufacturing, financial services, and beyond. Blue Prism has a drag-and-drop interface built around connectable objects containing actions and events, with a documented history of processes. The company was founded in 2001.

The digital workforce is built by the operational teams or accredited Blue Prism partners using their robotic process automation technology to rapidly build and deploy automations through leveraging the presentation layer of existing enterprise applications. The automations are configured and managed within an IT governed framework and operating model, which has been iteratively developed through numerous large scale and complex deployments.

UiPath is an RPA company that offers a platform for automating repetitive manual tasks. Thanks to the ease of use for its automation designer, UiPath's robots can operate with or without human supervision (help desks and call centers). Now based in New York, the company was founded in Bucharest, Romania, in 2005. The company raised $568 million in its latest Series D funding round and is one of the RPA giants with over $7 billion valuation.

SAP Intelligent Robotic Process Automation is a complete automation suite where software robots are designed to mimic humans by replacing manual clicks, interpreting text-heavy communications, or making process suggestions to end users for definable and repeatable business processes. SAP's offering incorporates machine learning and conversational AI alongside RPA.

Other startups worth observing in RPA domain are:

- WorkFusion,
- Pegasystems,
- Cognizant.

All of them are working on their proprietary software and heavily investing in AI. Large tech companies are also slowly entering the market, some of them like IBM collaborates with existing RPA providers (Automation Anywhere), others like Microsoft, try to develop their own set of tools.

Even though RPA companies are relatively big, there is still a place for newcomers. Startups looking to disrupt the RPA market should look towards reinforcement learning and recent breakthroughs in text processing. The space of RPA tools is big enough to welcome new players without stealing the business from established companies. Another potential direction for startups is to narrow down automation tools only to a particular business niche like law, logistics, or finance.

Having said that, RPA is yet to grow immensely, thanks to progress in machine learning. Most RPA systems are legacy solutions compared to what is currently possible with machine learning.

Image generation

Deepfakes are hyper-realistic AI-generated images and videos. They entered the mainstream, making real and fake media indiscernible. This shows another side of democratising AI: an easy availability for malicious use in disinformation and malware.

Media companies are the first to engage in using image generation.

At the end of December 2019, Snapchat acquired AI Factory, a Ukraine-based startup developing computer vision products, for $166M[43]. Snap had previously worked with AI Factory to power Cameos, a feature that enables users to insert their selfies into GIFs to create animated deepfakes. Snapchat Cameos are an alternative to Bitmoji for quickly conveying an emotion, reaction, or silly situation in Snapchat messages.

---

[43] https://techcrunch.com/2020/01/03/snapchat-quietly-acquired-ai-factory-the-company-behind-its-new-cameos-feature-for-166m/

TikTok, owned by ByteDance, is working on a similar feature: it has built technology to let you insert your face into videos starring someone else.[44]

Samsung engineers have developed realistic talking heads that can be generated from a single image, so AI can even put words in the mouth of the Mona Lisa.[45]

Hollywood also is betting on AI.

The cast of "The Irishman," Robert De Niro and Al Pacino, was digitally de-aged in the film using AI. Hollywood is heading towards "digitally resurrecting" actors from the '50s and '60s in films: supposedly James Dean is going to appear in one of the movies thanks to AI.[46]

Warners Bros. started a collaboration with Cinelytic[47] to use their comprehensive data and predictive analytics to guide decision-making at the greenlight stage. The integrated online platform can assess the value of a star and how much a film is expected to make in theaters and on other platforms. This means that AI has a say in what movies will be produced. A similar example is Scriptbook, a startup developing AI tools to analyse a script and try to predict whether it will be a hit

---

[44] https://techcrunch.com/2020/01/03/tiktok-deepfakes-face-swap/
[45] https://www.sciencealert.com/samsung-s-ai-can-now-generate-talking-heads-from-a-single-image
[46] https://www.foxbusiness.com/technology/james-deans-cgi-resurrection-raises-questions-about-dignity-of-dead-hollywood-actors
[47] https://www.hollywoodreporter.com/news/warner-bros-signs-deal-ai-driven-film-management-system-1268036

or a flop. Results seem promising.[48] To finish with the movie industry, Netflix estimates its recommendation engine to be crucial for its existence and worth over $1 billion.[49]

Fashion is also heavily investing in AI.

UK-based startup Superpersonal has created an app that will allow users to try on clothes virtually. Users feed the app basic information, including gender, height, and weight. The app then records the user's head movements. From this data, the app creates a virtual version of the user modeling clothes: great both for personal and commercial use.

The Echo Look is Amazon's "style assistant" that takes a photo of your outfit and makes fashion recommendations that are conveniently available for sale on Amazon.

Zao, a free deepfake face-swapping app that's able to place your likeness into scenes from hundreds of movies and TV shows after uploading just a single photograph, has gone viral in China.

On the other hand, solutions are needed to counter deepfakes used for malicious purposes. Two such examples are Sherlock AI and TruePic, which were created to detect deepfakes and verify content. Facebook, in collaboration with Microsoft, started Deepfake Detection Challenge to create benchmarks for evaluating deepfakes.

---

[48] https://www.scriptbook.io/#!/scriptbook/proof
[49] https://www.businessinsider.com/netflix-recommendation-engine-worth-1-billion-per-year-2016-6?r=US&IR=T

All in all, image generation will be an important route for the entertainment and fashion industries. Both are already experimenting heavily with deepfakes and image generation. Next come e-commerce and retail businesses, which will use image generation to improve customer experience, and go into the direction of hyperpersonalisation. Also, the media will be influenced by image generation, especially TV anchors - the world's first AI news anchor has already debuted in China.

Text generation and Chatbots

Text generation had experienced the most significant breakthrough in 2019 when OpenAI announced GPT-2. This Transformer-based model was able to generate coherent pieces of text on a large scale.

GPT-2[50] is a large transformer-based language model with 1.5 billion parameters, trained on a dataset of 8 million web pages. GPT-2 is trained with a simple objective: predict the next word, given all of the previous words within some text. The diversity of the dataset causes this simple goal to contain naturally occurring demonstrations of many tasks across diverse domains. GPT-2 is a direct scale-up of GPT, with more than 10X the parameters and trained on more than 10X the amount of data.

The whole 2019 was full of surprises when it comes to text generation models with Megatron from NVIDIA being 5 times

---

[50] https://openai.com/blog/better-language-models/

larger than GPT-2 and finally Turing-NLG from Microsoft being 10 times larger than GPT-2 (released in February 2020).

We are just beginning to experience the consequences of these breakthroughs:

- chatbots are getting much better,
- voice assistants are on the rise,
- tools for language understanding are getting better.

One example of a super-powered chatbot is Meena from Google.[51] Meena is an end-to-end, neural conversational model that learns to respond sensibly to a given conversational context.

In 2018 we saw Google Duplex, an assistant from Google, call a restaurant and book a table.[52] Similar tools are already in use in China, developed by Baidu and Alibaba.

Text generation tools are already used in customer service and support. In the form of chatbots, these tools can quickly assess a question, answer simpler ones and direct more complex to a human worker. This saves a lot of time by allowing human workers to focus on more involved and interesting cases, rather than constantly answering the same type of questions.

There is plenty of solutions available on the market which are easy to implement and don't require coding.

---

[51] https://ai.googleblog.com/2020/01/towards-conversational-agent-that-can.html
[52] https://www.youtube.com/watch?v=D5VN56jQMWM

On the other hand, the most complex ones are custom-made powered by machine learning and trained on proprietary internal data. The cost of entrance to text generation is still relatively high, especially compared to other domains of machine learning. That's not surprising as text understanding is one of the hardest areas of machine learning.

In general, applications of Natural Language Generation (NLG) vary from sales and marketing to market research and customer service. To name a few bigger startups in this domain:

Conversica's AI platform converts leads to sales opportunities via natural, two-way email conversations. It creates engaging conversations to boost your sales.

Persado Marketing Language Cloud delivers AI-generated language that resonates the most with your audience.

Acrolinx is in the content marketing and advertising sector. It aligns your content with your guidelines and uses automation for shortening your editorial process.

Narrative Science interprets and transforms your enterprise data into intelligent narratives like content for your website or analytic reports.

Automated Insights develops technology that automatically generates narratives on a massive scale that sound like a person crafted each one.

OneSpot generates personalized content after viewing a website user's history on the internet.

The opportunities for a content generation will only grow with time as this technology will become more mature. Together with Image Generation methods, companies will be able to automate their content production or at least radically save time on producing content.

AI-powered education

Education is also transformed by AI. Most of the innovations so far were on the side of running massive online classes. Companies like Coursera or edX are leading the way of online education, enrolling millions of students into courses from higher education institutions.

Nevertheless, more edtech companies are investing in machine learning solutions to track the progress of students and personalise their learning experience. AI promises global access to personalised education for anyone.

Advances in speech and text understanding allow AI to answer questions from students instantly, guiding them through the process along the way.

Reports from EdTechXGlobal and Ibis capital estimated that schools spent nearly $160 billion on education technology, or edtech, in 2016, and forecast spending to grow 17 percent annually through 2020. Also, private investments in educational technology increased by 32% in the last couple of years.

Coursera's online classes use machine learning to alert teachers when a large number of students make similar errors on an assignment, suggesting possible gaps in the teachers' lectures or course materials.

Another application of AI in education will come in the form of profiling students to divide them into groups according to their skills and the pace of learning. Collaboration.ai uses artificial intelligence to process data on each student's experience, knowledge, and capabilities and recommend group formations best suited for the learning objective. Machine learning can identify complementary skills that would maximize critical thinking and test students' capacity to adapt and collaborate.

Also, traditional universities are experimenting with Artificial Intelligence to improve student retention. Some schools are testing advanced analytics to identify students in trouble and offer them support before they drop out; for example, this is done by Civitas Learning and Salesforce.[53] The Salesforce tools use machine learning to recommend engagement strategies to improve graduation rates and minimise churn.

AI also helps grade students' assessments. Gradescope helps seamlessly administer and grade all of the assessments, whether online or in-class. Teachers save time grading and get a clear picture of how students are doing.

---

[53] https://www.salesforce.org/salesforce-org-civitas-learning-connect-insights-action-across-connected-campus/

Microsoft also does a lot to promote access to education: collaborating with schools, individual educators, and other companies. They are particularly keen on bringing AI to schools. Microsoft commissioned a report on education from IDC, which covered 509 higher education institutions in the US, and found that 99.4% of respondents say AI will be instrumental to their institution's competitiveness in the next three years. Furthermore, 15% called AI a "game-changer," and 54% have started to experiment with AI, while 38% have adopted AI as a core part of their business strategy.

At the University of New South Wales in Sydney, Australia, David Kellermann has built a question bot capable of answering questions and delivering past video lectures. The bot can also flag student questions for teaching assistants to follow up. What's more, it keeps getting better at its job as it's exposed to more and different questions over time.

Duolingo uses AI in its gamified lessons. The company reaches over 300 million users with more than 32 language courses—from French and Tamil to endangered languages such as Hawaiian and Navajo. You learn by completing short lessons, repeating those where you failed. The algorithms learn your speed of learning and suggest appropriate tasks to boost your learning.

China is also heavily investing in AI education. Adaptive learning is an education technology that can respond to a student's interactions in real-time by automatically providing the student with individual support. SquirelAI is the first AI-powered adaptive education provider in China. They provide personalized and high-quality K-12 after-school tutoring at an affordable price, addressing:

- lack of personalized attention in traditional classrooms,
- unequal distribution of educational opportunities.

HolonIQ[54] predicts that AI adoption in education will explode over the next five years and is expected to reach a global expenditure of $6b by 2025. Much of the growth will come from China, followed by the USA, together accounting for over half of global AI education spend.

This is good news for anyone interested in the education space. The 2020 remote work environment caused by lockdowns around the world is also changing how students engage with teachers. We have to wait to see how education will change, but definitely, in the upcoming years, we will witness a disruption of standard models of education that were dominant for the past hundreds of years. Thanks to AI and online learning, education will be democratised and freely available to anyone.

AI in Healthcare

Artificial Intelligence can already review health records and medical data with more speed and accuracy than humans. Thus AI in healthcare can significantly increase the accuracy and reduce the likelihood of human error in:

---

[54] https://www.holoniq.com/notes/2019-artificial-intelligence-global-education-report/

- diagnostics,
- treatment plans,
- overall patient care.

In the next years, we will see more and more doctors working closely with software, which will boost largely available help for patients, not only in developed countries but even in the most remote regions.

A good example here is Bosch Vivascope,[55] which is a cell-analysis platform using artificial intelligence to detect anomalies in biosamples. There are many regions of the world, where laboratory medicine is scarce. Sometimes there's only one pathologist to 1.5 million people in a region. There's often no one to examine blood for diseases and make a diagnosis. Two-thirds of the examinations are still carried out with a microscope, which is time-consuming. Vivascope can help those people in rural regions, preventing the spreading of diseases and boosting their overall health.

Cancer diagnoses

Artificial Intelligence is already being used to detect diseases more accurately than ever before. The AI program reliably interprets mammograms and translates patient data into diagnostic information 30 times faster than a human doctor, with 99% accuracy.[56]

---

[55] https://www.bosch.com/stories/vivascope-artificial-intelligence-medical-diagnosis/
[56] https://www.wired.co.uk/article/cancer-risk-ai-mammograms

A high proportion of mammograms yield false results, leading to 1 in 2 healthy women being told they have cancer. The use of AI helps reduce the need for unnecessary biopsies.

There are other examples of using AI in detecting cancer. Automated classification of skin lesions using images is a challenging task owing to the fine-grained variability in the appearance of skin lesions. In a 2017 Nature article, Esteva et al.[57] describe an AI system trained on a data set of 129,450 clinical images of 2,032 different diseases and compare its diagnostic performance against 21 board-certified dermatologists. The AI system could classify skin cancer at a level comparable to the dermatologists.

Google has used machine learning to improve the detectability of prostate cancer. It has achieved an overall accuracy of 70% when grading prostate cancer in prostatectomy specimens. The average accuracy achieved by US board-certified general pathologists in the study was 61%.[58]

MaxQ.AI is building towards AI-augmented healthcare through medical diagnostic solutions that help empower physicians around the world to prioritize better and identify life-threatening conditions such as stroke and traumatic brain injury in acute care settings.

Turbine.AI models how cancer works on the molecular level and tests millions of potential drugs with artificial intelligence.

---

[57] https://www.nature.com/articles/nature21056
[58] https://ai.googleblog.com/2018/11/improved-grading-of-prostate-cancer.html

There are plenty more startups in healthcare space diagnosing cancer thanks to progress in image recognition algorithms and access to vast data of scans. We're bound to see more applications of AI in cancer diagnosing and fighting it in the first phases.

General screening and general care

AI will be applied to the design and development of clinical trials, which is a labor-intensive and manual process. With a market size expected to hit $68.9 billion by 2026, optimizing the clinical trial workflows could help to reduce spending, lower costs, optimize processes. Already, AI-automated trial matching can integrate data from electronic health records, medical literature, and eligibility criteria from legislative bodies and learn how to interpret the trial requirements based on patient cases. In one IBM Watson Health™ study, AI-based identification cut the time required to screen patients for clinical trial eligibility by 78%.[59]

I have already mentioned Vivascope above. Boosting pathologists with AI is also a goal of PathAI startup.[60] PathAI is developing technology that assists pathologists in making rapid and accurate diagnoses for every patient, every time.

Screening goes beyond just diagnosing cancer, and the list grows longer with every day. Machine learning models were used to:

---

[59] https://www.ibm.com/blogs/watson-health/value-based-healthcare/
[60] https://www.pathai.com/what-we-do/

- Detect and classify cardiac arrhythmia using ECGs, achieving cardiologist-level performance.
- Reconstructing speech from neural activity in the auditory cortex.
- Prevent or manage diseases.
- Address unhealthy behaviors before people become patients (tracking diets, fitness routines, etc.).

DeepMind analyzed over 1 million anonymous eye scans to train itself to be able to identify the early signs of eye disease. For that, Google's DeepMind collaborated with NHS working with London's Moorfields Eye Hospital to develop a machine learning system that will detect the early signs of degenerative eye conditions that humans might miss. [61]

Another use case is detecting diabetic retinopathy from eye scans. This condition happens when high levels of blood sugar lead to damage in the blood vessels of the retina. Autonomous AI that instantly detects disease was created by IDX.[62]

With more data sources coming from our smartphones, smartwatches, laptops, camera, IoT devices, and so on, global organisations can track our behaviors better. Apart from privacy concerns you might have, the benefit would be an improvement in our health, thanks to monitoring early symptoms and suggesting behaviors that we should correct. You can already download various apps from Samsung or Apple, which monitor your health based on data coming from your smartphone

---

[61] https://www.independent.co.uk/life-style/gadgets-and-tech/google-deepmind-nhs-ai-eye-disease-early-signs-learn-a7120571.html
[62] https://www.eyediagnosis.co/

and smartwatch. With the more sophisticated technology, we will be able to prevent many strokes, heart failures, and other diseases.

More general solutions already exist. Babylon Health has been designed around a doctor's brain to provide accessible healthcare for millions. Their AI solution can understand and recognise the unique way that humans express their symptoms. Using this knowledge, combined with a patient's medical history and current symptoms, AI provides information on possible medical conditions and common treatments.[63]

A big segment of the health industry is related to care for elderly people. There are a lot of experiments using robots or VR with the idea of reducing loneliness and add a point of contact in emergency cases.

A different use case is applying machine learning to help people visually impaired navigate. AI is now able to identify objects and read a text, convert handwriting or printed text to digital text and read it aloud. Microsoft's Seeing AI used those techniques to bring a solution available in 70 countries free of charge. A similar solution is OrCam MyEye camera, which is mounted on standard glasses and converts what is seen into spoken output.

Thus AI can be a great tool to improve access for impaired or elderly people. We're yet to see this direction of research to develop, especially that going from a research phase to

---

[63] https://www.babylonhealth.com/ai

production can take time due to regulations that are required to be met.

Research and development

The path from the research lab to the end-user, which is a patient, is long and costly. California Biomedical Research Association estimates it takes an average of 12 years for a drug to go from the research lab to the patient and around $359M. Furthermore, only five in 5,000 of the drugs that begin preclinical testing ever make it to human testing, and just one of these five is ever approved for human usage.[64]

The greatest challenge today in pre-clinical drug discovery and development is identifying a drug candidate that is both effective and safe. It is a problem faced by researchers in every pharmaceutical company, whether small or large and in thousands of research institutions across the world.

Drug research and discovery is one of the more recent applications for AI. By directing the latest advances in AI to streamline the drug discovery and drug repurposing processes, there is the potential to significantly cut both the time to market for new drugs and their costs.

Genomic modeling is one of the domains ripe for disruption with AI. DeepMind has built Alphafold[65] to understand protein

---

[64] http://www.ca-biomed.org/pdf/media-kit/fact-sheets/CBRADrugDevelop.pdf
[65] https://deepmind.com/blog/article/AlphaFold-Using-AI-for-scientific-discovery

folding and determine the 3D structure of proteins. Their solution borrows concepts from natural language processing to predict distance and angle between amino acids. Understanding their structure and how they fold presents the opportunity to develop drugs for previously unknown targets.

This leap forward in drug discovery allows Relay Therapeutics to leverage the relationship between protein motion and function, creating opportunities to develop more effective therapies for multiple diseases.

Atomwise develops technology that uses a statistical approach that extracts the insights from millions of experimental affinity measurements and thousands of protein structures to predict the binding of small molecules to proteins. This tool makes it possible for chemists to pursue discovery, lead optimization, and toxicity predictions with precision and accuracy.

Exscientia is another startup using AI to discover new drugs. Exscientia's Centaur Chemist™ approach transforms drug discovery into a formalized set of moves and a system that learns strategy from human experts. Then AI algorithms can outperform expert human drug designers in the search for optimised drug compounds.

LabGenius is a biopharmaceutical company developing next-generation protein therapeutics using a machine learning-driven evolution engine, integrating machine learning, synthetic biology, and robotics. They use deep learning to explore protein fitness landscapes and improve multiple drug properties simultaneously.

At Insitro, which launched with $100M in VC financing, computational experts and biologists work together to create lab experiments and produce massive custom data sets. Then machine learning models find patterns to suggest new tests and potential therapies. Automated pipetting machines and other robotics tools reduce human error. Thanks to that Insitro can do experiments in a matter of weeks instead of years.[66]

In general, pharma is among the most willing to invest in AI, as drug research is expensive to carry on successfully. The costs of hiring a data science team are relatively low compared to the costs of developing even a single drug available commercially. Definitely, in the upcoming years, we will see breakthroughs in drug discovery coming from AI and other cutting edge technology, especially quantum computing is promising when it comes to applications in pharma.

Cybersecurity powered by AI

When it comes to our security in the digital world, AI is transforming both sides - it's both defending and attacking us. Its malicious uses can be tracked to hackers trying to get into our bank accounts, stealing precious information from corporates and governments, or simply cracking our social media accounts.

On the other hand, we have better and more reliable defense systems which, through ultra-personalization, allow us to

---

[66] https://www.forbes.com/sites/jilliandonfro/2019/11/11/daphne-koller-in-sitro-and-ai-powered-plan-to-discover-new-drugs/#6f47faf8763b

identify whether the agent is really what he claims to be, think about face-unlocking on phones, or determining who's typing by the speed of typing.

Yet, on the other hand, ultra-personalisation goes together with a lack of privacy and surveillance capitalism. It's often privacy versus security. Is there a way out?

More Cybersecurity AI startups are raising funds to defend us against hackers and malicious use of the software. Darktrace, a global machine learning company specialized in cyber defense, raised over $230M in total. It uses behavioral analytics to detect abnormal behavior in organizations automatically.

Some other notable cybersecurity startups using AI include:

- Cylance applies AI algorithms to predict, identify, and stop malware.
- ThetaRay uses AI to provide real-time detection of anomalies and unknown threats, especially in the financial sector and industry.

The malicious use of AI gets more sophisticated too. Criminals used artificial intelligence to impersonate a chief executive's voice and demand a fraudulent transfer of €220,000 in March 2019[67]. There were other cases like that.

---

[67] https://www.wsj.com/articles/fraudsters-use-ai-to-mimic-ceos-voice-in-unusual-cybercrime-case-11567157402

There's also a potential for using deepfakes to spread misinformation and influence public opinion. Fake news were largely used in political campaigns in the US in 2016 with massive reach thanks to Facebook (Cambridge Analytica scandal).

With lowering entry barriers, AI will be more often used by hackers in the upcoming years. This means that to protect ourselves and our companies, we will need to use AI-based solutions as well. The global cyberwar is yet to begin.

Climate Change

Climate is becoming more of an issue each year, with the weather becoming more extreme in various parts of the world. We've already passed a point where restrictions will suffice, and we need to proactively change the way we manufacture, consume, and live. AI will play a role in our fight for the climate. Not only algorithms already provide better analytics and actionable insights, but paired with advances in robotics AI will be able to help us transit into renewable energies, reducing waste and emissions of greenhouse gas.

The most visible effect of pollution is plastic floating in the oceans. It ends up in animals' stomachs leading to their death. This interrupts the food chain, influencing directly all other animals and humans alike and causing damage to the marine industry. Here comes Clear Blue Sea with FRED – the Floating Robot for Eliminating Debris. FRED is a solar-powered marine vessel capable of harvesting floating marine debris. Another example is a marine drone called the WasteShark cleaning up plastic waste off the coast of Devon in the United

Kingdom. Unmanned, autonomous vehicles can help with cleaning tasks where humans don't want or can't go.

Plastic in oceans is, of course, just the tip of an iceberg when it comes to climate. A group of researchers from various US institutions has prepared an in-depth guide on how machine learning can help tackle climate change.[68] The whole paper is over 100 pages long and is worth reading for anyone interested in how they can leverage AI to tackle climate change. The following summarises[69] some of the aspects the authors have mentioned throughout the paper, which is divided into the following sections:

Electricity Systems: Forecasting supply and demand, Improving scheduling and flexible demand, Accelerating materials science, Managing existing technologies, Accelerating fusion science, Reducing life-cycle fossil fuel emissions, Reducing system waste, Modeling emissions, Improving clean energy access, Approaching low-data settings.

Transportation: Understanding transportation data, Modeling demand, Shared mobility, Freight routing and consolidation, Alternatives to transport, Designing for efficiency, Autonomous vehicles, Electric vehicles, Alternative fuels, Passenger preferences, Enabling low-carbon options.

Buildings and Cities: Modeling building energy, Smart buildings, Modeling energy use across buildings, Gathering

---

[68] https://arxiv.org/pdf/1811.04551.pdf
[69] for the complete summary see: https://www.climatechange.ai/summaries

infrastructure data, Data for smart cities, Low-emissions infrastructure.

Industry: Reducing overproduction, Recommender systems, Reducing food waste, Climate-friendly construction, Climate-friendly chemicals, Adaptive control, Predictive maintenance, Using cleaner electricity.

Farms and Forests: Remote sensing of emissions, Precision agriculture, Monitoring peatlands, Estimating carbon stock, Automating afforestation, Managing forest fires, Reducing deforestation.

CO_2 Removal: Direct air capture, Sequestering CO_2, Understanding personal carbon footprint.

Climate Prediction: Data for climate models, Clouds and aerosols, Ice sheets and sea-level rise, Working with climate models, Storm tracking, Local forecasts.

Societal Impacts: Monitoring ecosystems, Monitoring biodiversity, Designing infrastructure, Maintaining infrastructure, Food security, Resilient livelihoods, Supporting displaced people, Assessing health risks, Managing epidemics, Disaster response.

Solar Geoengineering: Understanding and improving aerosols, Engineering a planetary control system, Modeling impacts.

As you can see, the list is pretty comprehensive. For each of those points, authors discuss what AI can and can't do, and what are current opportunities, what is being done and what's missing. If you're interested in any of these aspects of climate change, I highly suggest you go to the original paper.

On the other hand, looking from a general perspective, what AI enables in most of these cases is a superb capability to monitor data and predict/forecast events, even rare ones. We can better understand what our actions are doing to the climate, what we can improve, and more importantly how. Machine learning allows us to monitor vast amounts of data in real-time, from carbon footprint, gas emissions to plastic. Monitoring can then be used to engineer solutions that would minimise our bad influence on climate: like improving the efficiency of cities, predicting cyclones, making agriculture smart. These kinds of changes are already applied across every domain.

However, the problem with climate is often more political than economic. It boils down to how to implement changes in large organisations and countries which are far from the lean mindset of constantly changing startups. Definitely, competition and monetary incentives can play here a role, as AI will boost organisations which are ready to implement it and not only make them faster but also lower their overall costs considerably. We should make sure that this change will happen sooner than irreversible climate changes.

Games and Reinforcement Learning

Video games are an excellent simulation environment for training machine learning algorithms. Because of games' increasing complexity, games can be viewed as a model for our own reality. Learning how to play games is the first step to learn how to operate in real life. We value play as a way to learn for our children, and play is equally good for machines.

Reinforcement Learning (RL) techniques seem particularly well suited for games. The main focus of RL is to reward an algorithm when it completes a sub-task or moves in a good direction, and give it a penalty when it doesn't. This is the closest to raising a child with a set of rules on which it builds its world-view model. Reinforcement Learning agents learn tasks by trial and error. They must balance exploration (new behaviors) with exploitation (repeating past behaviors).

Experiments in Reinforcement Learning within games like Go, DOTA 2, or Quake III Capture the Flag show that without an explanation of rules, algorithms can figure out the game and learn complex strategies through self-play.

Over nearly 3 weeks in 2017[70], AI system Libratus played 120,000 hands of Texas hold'em against the human professionals and defeated four top human specialist professionals in heads-up no-limit Texas hold'em. In a study completed in December 2016 and involving 44,000 hands of poker, another AI system DeepStack defeated 11 professional poker players with only one outside the margin of statistical significance.[71]

A DeepMind agent reached human-level performance in a modified version of

---

[70] https://science.sciencemag.org/content/359/6374/418
[71] https://www.deepstack.ai/

Quake III Arena Capture the Flag, which is a complex, multi-agent environment and one of the canonical 3D first-person multiplayer games. The agents successfully cooperate with both artificial and human teammates and demonstrate high performance even when trained with reaction times comparable to human players.[72]

An interesting part of Deepmind's research, later also explored by OpenAI in their Hide&Seek project, is related to training multiple agents simultaneously. Deepmind researchers write that agents must learn from scratch to see, act, cooperate, and compete in new environments, all from a single signal per match: whether their team won or not. This is a challenging learning problem, and its solution is based on three general ideas in reinforcement learning:

- Instead of training a single agent, they trained a population of agents, which learn by playing with each other.
- Each agent in the trained population learns its own reward signal, which transfers to their own internal goals like capturing a flag. Then a two-tier optimisation process optimises agents' internal rewards for winning and uses RL on the internal rewards to deduce the agents' policies.
- Agents operate at two timescales, fast and slow, which boost their ability to use memory and generate consistent sequences of actions.

These agents trained by Deepmind showed human-like behaviors such as navigating, following, or defending. They have

---
[72] https://deepmind.com/blog/article/capture-the-flag-science

also exceeded the win-rate of strong human players both as teammates and as opponents.

OpenAI has trained AI systems on Dota 2[73]. Their OpenAI Five agents learned by playing over 10,000 years of games against itself. AI showed the ability to achieve pro-level performance, learn to cooperate with humans, and operate at scale. This was a great achievement as Dota 2 is an example of a multi-player collaborative game with fast-paced action.

Another achievement by Deepmind came with AlphaStar. AlphaStar is the first AI to reach the top league of StarCraft II without any game restrictions.[74] However these applications come at a cost, and it is estimated that training AlphaStar required $26M in computing resources.[75]

Probably the best known use case of Reinforcement Learning so far is AlphaGo Zero, which learns how to play Go from scratch to the level of top professionals, and beyond. The whole story is shown in a documentary called AlphaGo (highly recommended!).

This application was surprising because Go is a much more complex game than chess, equally renowned and old, with a whole ecosystem of fans, professional players, and broadcast, especially in Asia. Loss of Lee Sedol to AlphaGo came

---

[73] https://openai.com/projects/five/
[74] https://deepmind.com/blog/article/AlphaStar-Grandmaster-level-in-StarCraft-II-using-multi-agent-reinforcement-learning
[75] https://www.slideshare.net/StateofAIReport/state-of-ai-report-2019-151804430

as a shock to the Go community, and it was a moment that made the Chinese government invest heavily in AI, as Go is also very popular in China. In a sense, this was the Sputnik moment for the Chinese AI industry.

Reinforcement learning is also coming to the real world. OpenAI trained[76] a pair of neural networks to solve the Rubik's Cube with a human-like robot hand. The interesting part was that the neural networks were entirely trained in simulation, using the same reinforcement learning code as OpenAI Five with some improvements. The system can handle situations it never saw during training.

RL is often applied in autonomous vehicles, drones being a good example. Azure Drones is a civilian drone maker specializing in data capture and processing services for commercial applications. Skydio is a drone used to automatically follow you and record, great to record extreme sports' stunts or just a social gathering. A team of researchers at Stanford has also successfully deployed an autonomous helicopter.[77]

All in all, reinforcement learning is still mainly in the development phase. It seems that RL, together with text understanding, is the hardest subdomain in machine learning when it comes to the level of architecture complexity, amount of training needed, and expertise to deploy it. That's why we still have to wait to find scalable commercial applications of RL beyond games. But even within the game industry, there's a

---

[76] https://openai.com/blog/solving-rubiks-cube/
[77] http://heli.stanford.edu/

big potential when it comes to building AI agents, which could be good sparring partners for human players and guarantee an enjoyable game at any level.

Hardware and beyond

In this final section on Artificial Intelligence trends, I want to talk about hardware and physical devices related to AI: AI chips, IoT, smart cities, quantum computing. Let's have a look behind these buzzwords and see actual applications and opportunities.

It's worth noting that machine learning by itself, that is, as a set of learning algorithms, is not useful until you're able to provide it with enough computing power. That's why advances in computing power and general computation techniques are influencing AI progress. In 2019 and 2020, we could see that through Transformers models with billion parameters trained on millions of texts (GPT-2, Megatron, Turing-NLG). AlphaGo and AlphaStar from Deepmind needed millions of dollars in cutting edge computing power to achieve human-level performance in Go and StarCraft II, respectively. We can expect new amazing applications of deep learning will require even more computing power. That's why big tech companies are heavily investing in new AI chips and hardware, from TPU to quantum computing. Anything which has a chance to boost your AI algorithms and give you an advantage over your competitors is worth investing in.

On the other hand, computing power is not enough if you don't have data to feed to your algorithms. We are fairly good at collecting data online. Enterprises monitor their processes, and these are noted in CRMs, spreadsheets, and other tools that allow further extraction and processing of data. However, we only learn how and what to collect from the real world. Manufacturers invest in IoT to collect data within factories, municipalities install cameras and sensors to monitor human flow within cities, governments, and private companies look at satellite data, and the list goes on. In the future, we might expect centralized systems for monitoring data both in commercial and government use. Setting privacy issues aside, gathering data through monitoring will allow us to make our cities and organisations more smooth: less traffic, faster and more effective production. Of course, our privacy is a big issue, and the whole ethical side of implementing these solutions need to be thoroughly discussed.

IoT and Smart Cities

A smart city is a broad concept encompassing surveillance, mobility, and data infrastructure used together as data sources for machine learning algorithms. The goal of a smart city is to make living in a city a smoother, frictionless experience, just like buying online is nowadays.

Toronto Sidewalk Labs by Alphabet was probably the most comprehensive smart city project in the Western world. This Alphabet company aimed to build an entire neighborhood from the ground up, making it 'smart' in every aspect along the way. However, it was put on hold in 2020. As Sidewalk's CEO writes: "it has become too difficult to make the 12-acre project financially viable without sacrificing core parts of the plan we had developed together with Waterfront Toronto to build a truly inclusive, sustainable community."[78]

There are, however, a growing number of smart city projects around the world with ambitious plans, working by adding new sensors and new software to already existing infrastructure or building one from scratch:

- Toyota Woven City in Japan,
- ReGen Villages in California,
- Singapore as a whole.

China is also investing massively in smart cities. Surveillance is of key importance, and the government collaborates with private companies to attain its goals. Utilizing comprehensive real-time city data, Alibaba's City Brain[79] holistically optimizes urban public resources by instantly correcting defects in urban operations. This has led to numerous breakthroughs in urban government models, service models, and industrial development.

Reimagining cities for the future is a must with a growing population worldwide, congestion, pollution, and other civilization problems on the rise. Reimagining workplaces is also crucial for more effective and pleasant work. I have described how AI is applied in various domains in previous chapters to that end. What's left to be mentioned is that various sensors and devices which capture data are entering more workplaces

---

[78] https://medium.com/sidewalk-talk/why-were-no-longer-pursuing-the-quayside-project-and-what-s-next-for-sidewalk-labs-9a61de3fee3a
[79] https://www.alibabacloud.com/solutions/intelligence-brain/city

to monitor and analyse workflows, and eventually improve it. Industry IoT sensors are the largest part of this market, of course, because semi- and fully automated factories need access to real-time data to operate. However, more sensors are entering standard offices. Just think about motion sensors, occupancy sensors, cameras, and beacons. We're entering a new, interconnected world.

5G, Satellites and Artificial Intelligence

The vast amount of data coming from the physical and online world needs to be fed to machine learning algorithms to be useful for applications. And for that, we need a faster connection. Here comes 5G, a new generation of the industry standard. For comparison, 4G has a theoretical 100 megabits per second (Mbps) maximum speed, while 5G could achieve up to 10 gigabits per second (Gbps). Thus 5G is up to a hundred times faster than 4G. Moreover, it should also offer a more stable information transmission.

When it comes to 5G, China is far ahead of everybody else. However, the US and EU are actively pushing towards 5G. Huawei[80] has the most extensive declared 5G portfolio of patents, followed by Samsung, LG, and Nokia. Qualcomm and Intel are the largest US companies with 5G patents, while Sharp and NTT DOCOMO are the largest Japanese 5G patents declaring companies.

---

[80] https://www.iplytics.com/wp-content/uploads/2019/01/Who-Leads-the-5G-Patent-Race_2019.pdf

A patent advantage can position Huawei as the critical player in the upcoming 5G era, which would also include the whole ecosystem of network providers, device makers, and app developers. In Europe, the UK and Germany are using Huawei hardware, whereas the US looks for domestic alternatives.

Another contender for fast broadband connection is the Starlink project run by SpaceX and Elon Musk. SpaceX leverages its rocket building skills to deploy the world's most advanced broadband internet system powered by dozens of thousands of satellites (an initial plan mentioned 12,000 satellites, which was raised in 2019 to 42,000). The goal is to provide high-speed internet access across the globe. That will be a game-changer, especially for remote locations, where no Internet was available before. Hence Starlink is complementary to 5G, which will be mostly deployed in high population density areas.

Next-generation connectivity will allow us to gather data from all available sources and use it in machine learning applications.

AI Chips

Once the data is gathered and you have it ready for your machine learning algorithms, what's missing is computing power to handle the training of models. GPUs came as dominant hardware pieces for AI applications, with NVIDIA leading the race. However, since the new boom for AI, more hardware companies are entering the market of AI chips intending to speed up deep learning training.

Google came with TPU, a tensor processing unit, in 2016. TPUs are custom application-specific integrated circuits (ASIC) tailored for machine learning workloads on TensorFlow and potentially 15-30 times faster than GPUs (depending on to which model we compare them).

NVIDIA is not staying behind with constant innovation in GPUs and delivering commercial supercomputers for the office use like NVIDIA DGX station, which you can combine into DGX SuperPod.

Snapdragon 855 from Qualcomm is dedicated hardware and software designed to accelerate on-device AI. You can squeeze up to 7 teraOPS (7 trillion calculations per second) out of AI processing on Snapdragon 855.

Graphcore is a startup producing IPU (intelligent processing unit). Graphcore C2 IPU-Processor PCIe card achieves 3.7x higher throughput at 10x lower latency compared to a leading alternative processor. The company is backed by Microsoft.

It's no surprise that all tech giants either build their own AI chips or invest in startups building AI chips: Intel, Microsoft, Baidu, IBM, Samsung, Apple, LG, Amazon, Facebook. All are in this space, though for different reasons and different applications.

The most active startups in this space are Arm, Groq, SambaNova, and Wave Computing, among others. We're yet to see whether there will be a new standard for AI computations that would replace GPUs.

Quantum computing

Quantum computing is a new, revolutionary approach to computing with a goal to overcome Moore's Law and hugely boost computing speed. Quantum computers are based on qubits, which not only can be '0' or '1' like classical bits but can also be a superposition of those. A quantum phenomenon called entanglement allows interactions between any qubits in a quantum computer, whereas classical computers are limited to linear communication between neighboring bits. That roughly explains an exponential increase in power with a growing number of qubits in a quantum computer, compared to an only linear increase in power of classical computers.

Nevertheless, we are still early in the process of building and harnessing quantum physics for computing. Currently built quantum machines are not stable, have too much noise, and in general, are not ready to tackle commercial problems. However, a lot of research is being done in this space with investments coming from all tech giants: Google, Microsoft, IBM, and Fujitsu, among others. The most advanced company seems to be D-Wave when it comes to producing and selling actual quantum computers.

In recent years more and more startups are joining the race, building software solutions on already existing platforms. The hope is that with quantum computing, AI algorithms will gain enough power to identify patterns and derive insights from systems so complex that there just has not been enough classical computing power to model them. This includes problems like modeling chemical reactions, identifying compounds with similar chemical properties, and drug research and development. Startups tend to focus on particular niches and develop their own algorithms within the space, partnering with larger organisations to access to quantum computing.

Hybrid models look promising. They combine classical machine learning algorithms with quantum AI and has great potential for commercial applications. Interesting tests were done by Volkswagen together with D-Wave in the optimization space[81]. A Canadian startup Xanadu[82] used hybrid models to approach various machine learning problems, and their results also look promising. Worth noting is also Rigetti, a Californian startup both devising their own quantum chips and software ecosystem.

Quantum cloud computing war is yet to start once the technology is mature enough to be available commercially through the cloud. We should see significant investments and startup acquisitions coming from the likes of Google, Microsoft, IBM, and Amazon.

---

[81] https://www.dwavesys.com/media-coverage/volkswagen-optimizes-traffic-flow-quantum-computers
[82] https://pennylane.ai/

Machine Learning Trends

This chapter is similar to the previous one, where I looked at trends in Artificial Intelligence, except that here I want to accentuate actual algorithms being used. The goal here is mostly to list the most popular techniques and how they are going to be used in the future and possibly develop. Thus any decision maker should at least glance over some of those notions to get accustomed to how AI architecture looks like and what makes sense. So this chapter complements the previous one, which focuses on applications.

Natural Language Processing

2019 was especially significant for NLP. Various research breakthroughs happened, in particular the introduction of GPT-2 model for text generation by OpenAI. This model achieved never seen below accuracy in text generation, causing serious thoughts about security. The code of GPT-2 wasn't released all at once, OpenAI has opted for publishing a couple of models from weakest to strongest in 6 months span to ensure that it isn't used for malicious purposes.

Other research groups followed suit with Megatron (NVIDIA), BERT, Hugging Face, Allen Institute, culminating in Turing-NLG from Microsoft, the largest model in mid-2020. They all demonstrated that pre-trained language models could well solve various NLP tasks. All those models used massive datasets and considerable computing power. They were trained on large amounts of unlabeled text from the web (e.g. scraping articles from Reddit), and their underlying architecture was based on Transformers, an improvement on LSTMs which were popular in text generation tasks before.

In 2020 and beyond, we will see many applications of those methods: from chatbots to marketing and media. On the other hand, it seems like more data and more computing power will result in even better models. We currently don't know if there is a limit to Transformers' abilities and where it lies if it exists.

AutoML or automatic AI

We have a talent shortage globally in the AI industry. With the AI boom, every company needs someone to implement automation and harness data to improve business. One solution to this problem is democratization of AI education, another is AutoML. The goal of automatic machine learning is to discover necessary architecture for algorithms automatically and thus heavily reduce the amount of time needed to build and deploy new models as well as decrease the expertise required to use AI at all.

Recently AutoML tools for AI design have been gradually increasing in tasks like data preparation, training, model search, and feature engineering. Google offers Cloud AutoML, and other cloud platforms follow it by introducing ready-to-use machine learning models that self-optimize on your data and task. AutoML can be used in computer vision, video processing, translation, and NLP tasks.

Startups are also offering plug-and-play solutions, for example, Databricks, DataRobot, H2O, and RapidMiner.

AutoML not only answers talent shortage but also lowers cost and complexity. Designing neural networks is a time-consuming manual process even for the top talents, and AutoML can save their time on the least creative activities related to ML architecture design.

One-shot learning and transfer learning

If you don't have sufficient data to train deep learning algorithms, there are three ways to work around it: generate synthetic data, scrape/buy data from external sources or develop AI models that work well with small data.

Deep learning is very data-hungry — models are trained on huge sets of labeled data, e.g. millions of tagged animal images — and large amounts of labeled data are not available for specific applications. In such cases, training an AI model from scratch is often difficult, if not impossible.

As we've mentioned, one potential solution is to enlarge real datasets with synthetic data by generating more examples. This has been successfully used in autonomous driving, where autonomous vehicles drive millions of miles in photorealistic simulated environments that recreate situations like snowstorms and unusual pedestrian behavior and where acquiring real-world data is hard.

Similarly, researchers were experimenting with augmenting data in other scenarios where we lack sufficient real-world data like rare diseases. For example, NVIDIA did it by generating abnormal brain MRIs.[83] They have written in their paper: "Medical imaging data sets are often imbalanced as pathologic findings are generally rare, which introduces significant challenges when training deep learning models. We propose a method to generate synthetic abnormal MRI images with brain tumors by training a generative adversarial network."

Another way to circumvent the lack of data is to develop AI models that need smaller datasets to learn. In computer vision, we see more uses of transfer learning: taking a pre-trained algorithm and using it for a different task and data. Pre-trained models have also found their way to NLP with Transformers and GPT-2 done by OpenAI. The basic principle is to try to predict the next word in a sentence based on preceding words. We should expect more applications of transfer learning across every domain as it effectively lowers the cost of entry and running a commercial model.

In general, transfer learning is a technique that takes a neural network used for one task and applies it to another domain.

---

[83] https://news.developer.nvidia.com/ai-can-generate-synthetic-mris-to-advance-medical-research/

There are obvious problems in approaching a new problem with an old solution. Transfer learning techniques aim to overcome them. Say you have only 1,000 images of horses and want to build an algorithm for horse detection. By tapping into an existing neural network like ResNet, which was trained with more than 1 million images, you can right away get a good performance.

Reinforcement Learning

We talked about reinforcement learning a lot in the context of video games and simulations. When it comes to deploying reinforcement learning, the crucial part is to build a framework within which an RL agent can be trained.

Current most popular frameworks for reinforcement learning include:

– DeepMind Lab for 3D games like Quake,
– Arcade Learning Environment,
– Google Research Football,
– OpenAI Gym.

Reinforcement learning is still relatively new and undeveloped, and there's no one standard for benchmarking progress. However, RL is actively researched, and we should see a lot of breakthroughs in fundamental techniques and applications in upcoming years.

Computer Vision

With a new generation of hardware (AI chips, stronger GPUs), we see a lot of advances in image processing. Generative Adversarial Networks (GANs) since their introduction in 2015 became widespread and continue to surprise with their results. In particular, the next frontiers in image generation include commercial uses of GANs in the fashion and film industry; some we have discussed in the previous chapter.

In fashion, a standard process is organising a photo session for each new line of products. One needs high-quality photos with constraints on what's shown, namely a garment from a fashion designer. GANs could potentially be used to generate models on which fashion products are shown. Some experiments in this direction are already in place, but the whole problem - generating photorealistic images of models with particular pieces of clothes on them - seems still to be out of reach. Its solution will require both local and global GANs for managing the generation of images both on a micro and macro scale.

Another application frontier of GANs and other generation methods is video generation, where the ultimate problem is to generate a photorealistic video from a script. Currently, researches can't control the video. GANs are useful for generating 'generic' images and videos, and it's hard to impose constraints. With a better understanding of generative adversarial networks, we should expect movies entirely generated by AI, used both by Hollywood and marketing agencies. The end goal here is to generate everything using AI: script, actors, voices, and the movie itself. But for that result, we might wait at least another decade.

Fundamental concepts

Machine learning from a theoretical standpoint is still a relatively new domain, and there's a lot of theory missing, which would explain why certain fundamental concepts work in some cases and not in others. As of now, machine learning and data science are more practical and experimental sciences, similar to experimental physics, rather than state-and-prove pure mathematics.

Nevertheless, I firmly believe that we're going to see a more mathematical approach to neural networks, which would help clarify fundamental concepts. Such a theory would likely be within probability theory with elements of dynamical systems (training dynamics), representation theory (feature engineering, representation characteristics), and probably much more. As such, it would find a considerable appeal among mathematicians and theoretical computer scientists.

Currently, we don't even know how to answer the basic questions, like:

- how to select models for a particular problem and dataset,
- what influences training dynamics of a model,
- how neural networks represent data and what representation characteristics are.

We often can only answer these questions in particular scenarios, on limited real-world data, also using our common sense or expert knowledge about the world, and there's no one universal answer. It seems that modeling neural networks and their dynamics is a hard mathematical problem in itself and should be more researched in the near future.

Another reason for understanding fundamental machine learning concepts mathematically is a potential application to transfer learning, which in itself is the best way toward general artificial intelligence. Understanding neural networks' features like training dynamics, representation characteristics, model selection would allow us to generalize methods and use them across multiple domains, significant progress towards better transfer learning methods.

Pushing boundaries of machine learning

Finally, various alternative approaches emerged in recent years when it comes to model architectures, training, or even what a neural network should be. As I've written above, we're still early in the process of understanding machine learning and its applications. That's why each year brings breakthroughs, and it will stay so for the foreseeable future.

In this section, I've gathered concepts that push boundaries and are actively tested. Some of them might need years to fully blossom, while others would never make it out of research labs. Here are the top 4 trends in machine learning to watch in the upcoming years:

1. **Graph Neural Networks**
2. **Bayesian Deep Learning**
3. **Active Learning**
4. **Federated Learning**

Graph Neural Networks[84] are deep learning methods that operate on graphs. A graph is a data structure that models a set of objects (nodes) and their relationships (edges). Standard neural networks like CNNs and RNNs cannot handle the graph input properly, while understanding graphs is crucial in modeling more complex behaviors between objects. That's why graph neural networks are worth investigating. A similar concept that also tries to model hierarchical relationships better is Capsule Neural Networks.

The use of Bayesian techniques in deep learning is not new, however, recent advances in the field seem to yield many new exciting results. Bayesian Deep Learning is a way to achieve state-of-the-art results while also controlling the uncertainty of deep learning models. This is an important concept because it boils down to being able to pinpoint what an ML model doesn't know. If you train a dog/cat classifier and then feed a photo of a truck, the model should be certain that it doesn't know what it is, rather than make a random prediction.

Active learning is a machine learning algorithm that can interactively query an information source (e.g. user) to label new data points with the desired outputs. Or in other words, it can demand what it wants to learn next or just choose a subset of a dataset on which it wants to tune itself. Active learning comes as part of a larger movement to experiment with how the training process happens and how to make it more accurate.

---

[84] https://arxiv.org/pdf/1812.08434.pdf

Federated learning is an approach to learning where data is kept on separated mobile devices or servers without exchanging data samples. This is different from a classical approach that is centralized, and learning happens in one place on all data samples. This looks like a promising approach to building common, stronger models without breaching the privacy of data, and it should allow for commercial collaborations even among competitors. A startup Owkin[85] used federated learning to train machine learning models on data coming from multiple hospitals, preserving the privacy and security of each organisation.

Altogether these concepts lie at the boundary of what's possible in machine learning. We shall see in the upcoming years how they influence commercial applications. One thing is sure, AI will have a lot of surprises for us in the near future. It's time to embrace them as a society.

---

[85] https://owkin.com/federated-learning/

AI, Politics and Society

AI became a large part of our modern world, and it's hard to overestimate its influence on our daily life. Whether you google, ask for directions, scroll social media, watch Netflix - machine learning algorithms are behind every daily task.

US presidential elections in 2016 brought malicious use of harvesting data and privacy issues to the public. This resulted in Mark Zuckerberg, Facebook CEO, testifying before Congress, and in general more scrutiny towards the whole tech community. Silicon Valley ten years ago still seemed like a promised land. Ten years later, books like "The Age of Surveillance Capitalism" of Shoshana Zuboff point towards imperfections and inherent flaws in the California startup ecosystem.

That's why when introducing AI to organisations, communities, or societies as a whole, we need to clearly state our goals and explain what AI can and can't do. People should not worry about their jobs, or if they are directly influenced by automation, they should have access to retraining and education to remain relevant to the job market. AI will augment human capabilities, and the most likely scenario for our future is human-machine collaboration on every level, which would result in more effective and more pleasant work. The tedious, repetitive part will be taken care of by machines, while human workers will focus on original, creative jobs.

However, for this to happen, AI has to be democratised and by that, I mean we need to democratise access to AI tools, AI education, and computing power. The broader the workforce that can use AI, the better for our future and stability. That's why regulating AI business is vital to avoid monopolies and make sure that everyone can play a role in this booming industry, which influences every other sector.

It's worth mentioning that even jobs that rely on empathy and reading emotions are not immune to AI automation. I've discussed an example of a machine winning in Texas Hold-em, where bluffing is a common tactic, and one not only needs to count well but also recognise human emotions to win. Thus it is possible that AI will be able to read our emotions better than we do ourselves.

On the other hand, the role of the human will shift towards steering and applying AI to problems that are the most relevant and guiding its steps to a solution.

It's interesting to note how global news coverage of Artificial Intelligence has been growing in recent years. From the first mentions of breakthroughs to discussions of ethics, for example, about autonomous vehicles or weapons. It is essential to regularly educate the general public about possible opportunities and dangers of AI, and discuss with honesty what it can and can't do. This way, we will be all prepared for the inevitable changes that AI has for us in the near future.

AI for social good

Artificial Intelligence can do a lot of social good if it is applied wisely. Automatic analysis and insights in real-time deployed in critical areas can help:

- minimise the damage done by earthquakes, cyclones, and other extreme weather;
- guide blind people;
- personalise education to anyone anywhere;
- lower costs of drugs;
- decrease loneliness among the elderly;

and much more. However, this will require a considerable effort from the research community, entreprises, and regulators to make the whole AI ecosystem work together.

With AI being applied in each domain of our life, it's worth thinking about general social issues that might be solved using AI. McKinsey in their AI social report[86] mapped them into the following categories:

Crisis response: Disease outbreak, Migration crises, Natural and human-made disasters, Search and rescue missions.

---

[86] https://www.mckinsey.com/~/media/McKinsey/Featured%20Insights/Artificial%20Intelligence/Applying%20artificial%20intelligence%20for%20social%20good/MGI-Applying-AI-for-social-good-Discussion-paper-Dec-2018.ashx

Economic empowerment: Agricultural quality and yield, Financial inclusion, Initiatives for economic growth, Labor supply and demand matching.

Education: Access and completion of education, Maximizing student achievement, Teacher and administration productivity.

Environment: Animal and plant conservation, Climate change and adaptation, Energy efficiency and sustainability, Land, air, and water conservation.

Equality and inclusion: Accessibility and disabilities, Marginalized communities.

Health and hunger: Treatment delivery, Prediction and prevention, Treatment and long-term care, Mental wellness, Hunger.

Information: Verification and validation, Fake news, Polarization.

Infrastructure management: Energy, Real estate, Transportation, Urban planning, Water and waste management.

Public and social sector: Effective management of the public sector, Effective management of the social sector, Fundraising, Public finance management, Services to citizens, Transparency.

Security and justice: Harm prevention, Fair prosecution, Policing.

We can map these AI social goals directly with UN Sustainable Development goals which are:

- Life below water,
- Affordable and clean energy,
- Clean water and sanitation,
- Responsible consumption and production,
- Sustainable cities and communities,
- Gender equality,
- Partnerships for the goals,
- Zero hunger,
- Decent work and economic growth,
- Climate action,
- Reduced inequalities,
- Industry, innovation, and infrastructure,
- No poverty,
- Life on land,
- Quality education,
- Peace, justice, and strong institutions,
- Good health and well-being.

Can AI solve all our problems? Not by itself. AI is just a tool and we will need to collaborate across organisations, societies, and nations to build our common AI future which would serve everyone and which would be inclusive.

Public programs

Realising the importance of AI, governments started joining the race as well. In recent years dozens of countries drafted their AI strategies, which usually concentrated on boosting the local startup ecosystem and incentivising large enterprises on R&D research.

The biggest AI spender in the world seems to be China, which some estimates to spend around $70 billion up to 2020 on AI-related research and businesses.[87] The precise estimates are hard to make due to lack of transparency, however, the annual AI budget of China seems to be within the range of a couple to a dozen billion dollars.[88] USA seems to have a similar yearly budget level, though due to US-China competition, we should see a growing level of investments in AI in upcoming years, as this technology is of strategic importance.

In general, 2019 was the biggest year in funding, both federal and private, for artificial intelligence ventures yet, and 2020 should be even bigger. This trend should continue as the technology matures.

In the USA, in June 2019[89], the White House's AI R&D Strategic Plan defined several key areas of priority focus. The main 8 strategic priorities were:

1. continued long-term investments in AI;
2. developing effective methods for human-AI collaboration;
3. understanding and addressing the ethical, legal, and societal implications for AI;

---

[87] https://www.technologyreview.com/2019/12/05/65019/china-us-ai-military-spending/
[88] https://cset.georgetown.edu/wp-content/uploads/Chinese-Public-AI-RD-Spending-Provisional-Findings-2.pdf
[89] https://www.whitehouse.gov/wp-content/uploads/2019/06/National-AI-Research-and-Development-Strategic-Plan-2019-Update-June-2019.pdf

4. ensuring the safety and security of AI;
5. developing shared public datasets and environments for AI training and testing;
6. measuring and evaluating AI technologies through standards and benchmark;
7. better understanding the National AI R&D workforce needs;
8. expanding public-private partnerships to accelerate AI advances.

On the other hand, China launched its national program in 2017, with a goal to become the global leader in AI by 2030.

European countries are also joining this AI arms race, but with much more humble budgets. In 2018 France unveiled €1.5B plan to transform France into a global leader in AI. The main points of the plan were to launch a network of AI research institutes, have an open data policy to boost the adoption of AI, have a regulatory and financial framework for local companies, introduce ethical regulations.

In 2018 Germany allocated €3B for investment in AI R&D in its AI national strategy, with similar goals to French ones.

As a whole European Union also allocates funds to AI, which should reach €1.5B for the period 2018-2020 in its Horizon 2020 program. The goal is to:

– connect AI research centers across Europe,
– improve access to relevant AI resources in the EU for all users by a creating AI-on-demand platform,

− support the development of AI applications in key sectors.

Not only are countries allocating budgets to AI, but also cities strive to become AI hubs and attract top talents. There are various initiatives and strategies to meet these goals like:

− developing infrastructure,
− tax incentives for companies,
− investing in education and research,
− an easier path to implementation of AI and city-startup collaborations,
− regulatory frameworks.

All in all, through these programs around the world, the public sector tries to join the AI race and make sure that particular countries and cities stay relevant in the global technological economy. Equal access to AI is not given and has to be created by smart regulations, partnerships, and incentives. That's why it's crucial to educate policy-makers and decision-makers in the public sector so that in the new AI world, everyone will have the same chance of succeeding.

Ethics and Regulations

AI systems raise a variety of ethical and regulatory challenges. However, observing public discussion as well as governmental and academic debates, it seems that we're going in a good direction. Awareness of these problems is growing, and more funds are allocated to make sure that everyone has the same access to technology.

Most common challenges which appear in the context of AI are:

1. Interpretability and explainability, especially when it comes to AI-driven decision making;
2. Transparency, fairness, and accountability;
3. Democratisation of AI: diversity, inclusion;
4. Automation and job loss;
5. Data privacy and security;
6. Reliability and certainty of models;
7. Sustainability;
8. Compliance;
9. Human control.

Organisation for Economic Co-operation and Development (OECD) has drafted the OECD Principles on Artificial Intelligence[90] to promote AI that is trustworthy and respects human rights and democratic values. The following principles are recommended by OECD to build trustworthy AI systems:

- AI should benefit people and the planet by driving inclusive growth, sustainable development, and well-being.
- AI systems should be designed in a way that respects the law, human rights, democratic values, and diversity, and they should include appropriate safeguards to ensure a fair and just society.
- There should be transparency and responsible disclosure around AI systems to ensure that people understand AI-based outcomes and can challenge them.

---

[90] https://www.oecd.org/going-digital/ai/principles/

- AI systems must function in a robust, secure, and safe way throughout their life cycles, and potential risks should be continually assessed and managed.
- Organisations and individuals developing, deploying, or operating AI systems should be held accountable for their proper functioning in line with the above principles.

Consistent with these value-based principles, the OECD provides five recommendations to governments:

- Facilitate public and private investment in research and development to boost innovation in trustworthy AI.
- Foster accessible AI ecosystems with digital infrastructure and technologies and mechanisms to share data and knowledge.
- Ensure a policy framework that will open the way to deployment of trustworthy AI systems.
- Empower people with AI skills and support workers for a fair transition to AI-enhanced jobs.
- Co-operate across borders and sectors to progress on responsible stewardship of trustworthy AI.

The growing role of AI in our lives asks for better regulations. Old regulations must be updated to account for the transformative role AI can have on any business, organisation, and individual. Many countries have already realised that and national AI strategies explicitly mention the role of good regulatory frameworks for building trustworthy AI systems.

Risks of using AI

Developing Artificial Intelligence is not without risk. One of the biggest risks is that machine learning algorithms will be used maliciously to harm individuals, organisations, and society. We have already discussed how deepfakes and fake news can be created at scale using recent deep learning breakthroughs. That's why it's important to know how we can defend ourselves and what to look for.

Another risk is the displacement of the workforce or, in other words, the scale at which people could lose jobs due to automation. With AI becoming more sophisticated, it might be hard to find new job openings for less skilled staff. That's why it's crucial to democratise access to AI and technological education so that anyone can enter the job market again. This concerns not only physical jobs but also office jobs, which are also under attack from AI systems like RPAs we have discussed.

Yet another risk of using AI is the lack of transparency and bias in models. Machine learning models are trained on data provided by people and, as such, can inadvertently inherit biases in data provided. Imagine you've built an AI model for college admissions automated. If you've trained it on past data, then the chances are it's far from today's diversity standards, and it is biased towards students similar to alumni. This is why transparency and explainability of models are essential. We want to know why AI makes a particular decision.

Uncertainty of models is a risk that arises when we deal with sensitive data like medical data or crisis response. We can't rely on models that are not certain of their predictions. In other words, models have to be trained to account for what they don't know instead of always making predictions even if it's outside of the scope of their expertise.

Putting it all together, we can extract four categories of risks:

- the risk of malicious use of AI,
- the risk of negative impact on the job market and workers,
- the risk of bias and lack of transparency,
- the risk of privacy violation.

As a rule of thumb, the more sensitive data we deal with, the more cautious we should be about deploying AI. As machine learning is a statistical method, we should decide on how much risk of bias we allow, how certain AI should be, and how explainable. Each of these components increases the difficulty of building a compliant AI model able to solve the problem.

Summing up, AI can be a great tool to foster growth and build the wealth of a society, but one should be careful with applying it on a massive scale. Good regulations, together with consistent strategies, will help in using technology to our benefit. Policymakers need to balance between fostering AI growth and managing risks associated with it. As we have already discussed, AI strategy should account for democratisation, that is: accountability, explainability, and transparency while remaining secure and trustworthy. There's still a lot to do when it comes to establishing standards in ethics, regulations, and access. AI can be hugely beneficial to our society as well as it can do harm. It depends on us and our decisions. Our goal should not be to constrain the adoption of AI, but rather to encourage its safe use for social good.

Future of Artificial Intelligence

My goal in writing this book was to show the practical side of Artificial Intelligence and convey the feeling that it can be used in your business right now, whether you work at a large enterprise, run your own startup or you're a freelancer. In this final chapter, I want to focus on what's awaiting us in the future and discuss some issues related to why AI was so hyped in the first place.

Knowing what to expect is crucial if you want to prepare for the next decade or the next century. At least if that's still possible as changes occur faster than ever before. This exponential growth might stay for longer if automated machine learning (autoML) solutions became implemented on a large scale, allowing algorithms to tune themselves on the spot. As more jobs are being delegated to machines, it's worth asking whether humans will be at all necessary when it comes to work. There's no easy answer to that.

We are all cyborgs

A cyborg, as we know it from sci-fi, is a mix of human and a machine. Cyborgs are depicted in comic books, in sci-fi movies and video games and still seem a thing from a distant future. However, we are all cyborgs already. Most of our computational and communicational power, as well as our memory, is digitized and exists on the cloud or in our smartphone. Most of us have our smartphone within a hand reach for 95% time of the day, and we feel uncomfortable without it. We also feel inconvenient about a bad connection to the web or no wi-fi at all. That's how closely attached we have become to our devices.

This trend of becoming one with our devices will only grow stronger in the years to come. New generations will not know the world without the Internet, tablets, smartphones, laptops, and all the other devices, which make our life more comfortable and smoother. Technology is making our lives more convenient, and we're happy to embrace it.

That's why it seems natural (sic!) that we're going to become even more attached to our devices. Think about it this way: if there was a quick, non-painful process to implement smartphone capabilities within your body so that you won't need any external device to call, chat, surf the web, would you do it? Probably yes.

Artificial General Intelligence

In this book, I have depicted AI as an utterly practical framework for solving problems. However, a lot of people, when they think about AI, think about some powerful being, independent and intending to destroy the human race (e.g. Terminator), which is far from any predictable scenario. If AI destroys us, it'd be because we will use it as a weapon against each other.

Nevertheless, there is a concept of Artificial General Intelligence (AGI), a constructed entity capable of any menial task humans could do and performing it at least as well as humans do. AGI is the end goal of all AI research, the ultimate prize for solving machine learning problems. We don't know yet how to get there or even if it's even possible, but if it is, then that will be the greatest discovery of humankind ever made and also probably the last one. With enough computing power AGI will be capable of doing research by itself, faster and better than any team of researchers. Moreover, it will be able to deploy its own research right away, growing only stronger and faster. It will be a single entity able to dominate any domain within a short amount of time. Depending on your views on humankind and our future, that might be a scary or an optimistic vision. Elon Musk is one of the strongest advocates of controlling AI research because of the possibility of creation AGI within our lifetime. The malicious use of AGI would probably mean the utter destruction of everything we know. On the other hand, the safe and beneficial use of AGI would result in an amazing growth of the human race. That's why it's of utmost importance to make sure that AGI will be available to good agents, which would operate with a goal to benefit humankind.

We don't know how far we are from AGI currently. We could be hundreds of years away, or we could be 20 years away. But we shouldn't take risks here. Artificial General Intelligence is just a concept, but the transformative power of AI is real and is currently changing how we live and interact with each other. With or without AGI, we should strive for safe and beneficial use of AI systems, democratising access to AI and technological education, and making sure our tech culture is inclusive and open to diversity. Only this way we can ensure that AI will bring a bright future for humankind, rather than an apocalyptic dystopia.

Choices we make today will influence our future like never before.

Printed in Great Britain
by Amazon